Alan Gilbert

The Everyday Life of Design

Winter Editions, 2024

TABLE OF CONTENTS

LETTERS TO THE FUTURE

Time capsule   13
Not even at the beach   13
Free for all   15
Naming the constellations   16
Planetary love song   18
Horizon line   19
Species   21
But it won't stop the war   22
Not in service   25
Fire in the hole   26
Eyes on the exit   28
Next of kin   29
Gratuitous violence   30
Rules of the game   31
Multiple choice   33
Smoke and mirrors   35
Easy money   36
Take it or leave it   37
Holes in the surface   38
Begin again   39
Drifting to starlight   41
Go long   42
Rounding the corner   56
Butterfly on the breeze   58
Breaking news   59
Neon catastrophe   60
Coming to America   62
Difference in the same   65
Capture the flag   66
Full disclosure   67
Enough said   69
Deep shine   69

TANGLE OF WISHES

Kindred spirits   71
Dirty vinyl. Juicy fruit.   72
The war at home   73
Selfie in a convex mirror   74
Borrowed time   77
The dark net   77
The depressed therapist   80
The heart is heavy lifting   82
Begging to differ   83
Constitutional crisis   85
Pick of the litter   89
Worse than normal   90
Going over the wall   91
The foundlings   92
Soft targets   94
Open season   95
Untitled   97
Eviction notice   97
Between two points   98
A series of small favors   101
Postcards from paradise   102
Shelter from the storm (found poem)   103
Product placement   103
Cavity creep   106

DAMAGE IS DONE

Trees for the forest   109
Open all night   110
The courtesy interview   111
Lake of dreams   113
State of the union   125
Bent to the line   127
Flushing the lungs   128
Snap to grid   129
The passenger   130

Code switch   *132*
Swarm   *134*
Help wanted   *138*
Business as usual   *139*
Old wine in new bottles   *140*
Levitate the Pentagon   *142*
Listening in   *143*
Invisible script   *144*
Everybody in my feed   *145*
So much parade   *150*
Going off script   *151*
Attention span   *153*
More bang for the buck   *153*
A new hope   *155*
Contrapuntal   *157*
The dollar and the jugular   *158*
Loose cannon   *163*
Trouble in mind   *164*
One day at a time   *166*
It is always darkest right before the dawn   *167*
People, places, and things   *169*
Fight or flight   *170*

ORGAN DONOR
No child left behind   *172*
The crass menagerie   *172*
Dark waters   *173*
Speed dating for desiring machines   *175*
The crowd of unknowing   *176*
Blister pack   *177*
Whatever falls on the tracks is not as valuable as you are   *178*
Almost working   *180*
Faulty logic   *181*
Morning breath   *181*
Spider walk   *183*
Crosstalk   *184*

All this debris is starting to clog the system   *186*
Ordering off the menu   *187*
Cleaning up the toxic assets   *188*
The widow's claim   *190*
A winter light feeds just the same   *191*
Family resemblances   *193*
Happy cul-de-sac   *195*
Common economic indicators   *196*
Ticket to ride   *199*
Mercury in retrograde   *200*
Split the difference   *202*
A true story   if you believe it   *203*
The alchemy of morning   *204*
Push back at it   *206*
Breaking and entering   *207*
The carnivore's dilemma   *208*
Dedication   *209*
The pastoral is inside you   *210*
Future tense   *212*
Curious George goes to the beach   *213*
The environmental movement   *215*

DOCKING BAY

Cost of living   *215*
Dumb luck   *217*
Discontinuous signal   *220*
I love a parade   *221*
Price of admittance   *223*
The fast and the furious   *224*
The third way   *225*
A little haunting is a sweet pain   *226*
Trees and their tender maintenance   *227*
Memorial for the memorials   *228*
Campfires for DUMMIES®   *230*
Afternoon delight   *231*
Sonic warfare   *232*

Evening wear   234
Letter of the law   235
Ghosts that pursue us   236
Public hotel   237
The plastic chandelier   241
Lay of the land   243
Dry goods   244
Fairytales of the Late Holocene   246
Intelligence gathering   247
Revenge of the cheerleaders   249
Field guide   251

LOST IN THE GARDEN

Echoes   252
Puncture wound   267
For love and money   268
Song to the cypress   270
Shallow water skiff   271
Data dump   272
More fire   274
Funnel vision   275
Jawbone of an ass   277
The four seasons   279
Splashes and plops   280
Capillary   281
Direct deposit   283
Location scout   284
Ever given   286
Close to the bone   287
Speechsong   289
Last one standing   290

Acknowledgments   307

THE EVERYDAY LIFE OF DESIGN

LETTERS TO THE FUTURE

TIME CAPSULE

We wait for the medicine to take effect
when everything is at capacity
like an emotional spending spree,
all swollen heart and empty pockets.

We made a chair from some sticks
and the box we used to move the dishes,
but, please, just take it all away.
We need to leave a little land
for the fox to roam.

One noise drowns out another,
as voices get lost in the transmission,
    the transmission lost in the night,
        the night lost in you.
How did we get so restless?

Then one bird came back,
and we were grateful,
a sparrow's tiny feet clutching a thin branch.
We knew the end hadn't arrived just yet.

NOT EVEN AT THE BEACH

My online presence is an inflatable dog balloon
floating in a seal pool at the zoo.
At least summer is around the corner,
but then we'll be complaining about the heat.
Little seed: The grass will grow over it,

or the sands will cover it; the birds will ignore it,
or the flames will destroy it.
It was hard to keep the shrimp cocktail fresh
after we bought it on sale,
but those cupcakes might last forever—
such are the marvels of technology
waiting to swap us out.

We hear voices coming from the kitchen,
although we might also call them yelling
while we stand frozen in place,
a small patch of green and sunlight somewhere else.
When the sewers backed up
we went in search of bar stools.
I forget what happened in the first Avengers movie,
but I bet it was really cool.
There's a rhythm to every encounter—
just ask the ducks dodging the bobbing life rafts
or the fireman who had to go back and get his hat,
like a song that stops you in your tracks.

Maybe that's why I can't see ahead on this road,
and the deer would prefer to be left alone,
but here I come with a bag full of sugar cubes,
chewing a few as I go while checking my phone
for the cheapest shampoo
because my head could use a good rinse.
What are the narratives we tell ourselves?
The car ended up on the sidewalk,
denting the baby stroller's front spokes.
We've always been here before,
though I'd prefer it where the clocks don't work,
the night slowly encroaching upon us.

FREE FOR ALL

It would be better if the piñata was filled with lottery tickets
and I could scratch them off with the hitting stick.
Instead, I'm a paddleboat operator in a desert
after a sandstorm swallowed the landscape,
leaving behind bent sage and tarnished spoons
we used to scoop a path to wherever sorrow ends,
but only on a flat earth. No wonder we're always
hungry, and skydiving at night became our best option.

For many years, my mother sat under a dark moon,
as if the chair was made of stone or the ghost
of a crow croaked the words. Maybe that's why
I had to let everything go, especially after I lost
my internet connection and bought breakfast
at the gas station where the microwave was broken.
It took a while for the frozen meal to thaw,
its eggs first lifted from beneath a surly chicken.

Sometimes I feel a weird, crazy joy, and not only
when you pack a slice of melon with my lunch.
Almost every dog needs a walk, including us,
but I can download an app for that. Just don't
train me in a crate or sell me a ship beneath the sea,
because I used to have connections to the mob
across the street, although these days it's mostly
stealing office supplies with a dump truck.

The warm days are getting longer, so cancel my
membership in the huddle-up club. We're trying
to travel light, except the shadows cling to me.
The only monitoring I require is a spell check.
Free the robots. My circus is complete. Green trees
line a different river, although I wouldn't call it

a foreign shore with its collection of motorboats
and I need a drink whenever the ceiling closes.

Soon we were back on the road, not home
preparing the biscuit mix, leaving in little lumps
and the sirens outside: three loud blasts signal
an ambulance; five mean fire; two and I'm staying
under the covers because Iron Man needs
a new heart. I never gave up, and then I did,
but all of that uncertainty provided a little hope,
otherwise known as a chance to start over.

One of these days I'll make a comeback. Save me
a spot on the couch we took from the waiting room
after our doctor went out of business. I forgot
to include the moral uplift here in the end days
of the human and all that work in the garden
to have a tiny plot. We take the curtains down,
which lets the sun in, but now we can't sleep,
like keeping the basket and not what's in it.

NAMING THE CONSTELLATIONS

The plumber came for the clog while I was busy sneezing
on my sleeve and crushing ice cubes in the blender
with a headache, which means that ball of grease

and wet wipes will have to stay, lodged between
the preschool and the sewer, like feeling short of breath
when someone starts screaming. That's when I get out

my wayward map of the stars, away from all the madness
at home, except its cry is lodged in my soul like a squirrel
and its biggest nut as birds crisscross a pale-blue sky

called wonder, my face to the sun today, if only for a while.
Later, we'll make a sandwich, then push our clothes
to the laundromat with one of those folding metal carts

grannies find convenient, left rear wheel wobbling
the whole way, even in reverse when we didn't think
we'd make it. We still haven't. Or maybe we embarrassed

ourselves on Facebook despite getting all those Likes.
Don't troll me when I can do it myself. Who's in charge
here, anyway? The houses look empty, but that's my mess

in the other room next to the empty planter and tray tables
we balanced on our knees while watching TV because
sometimes you hear the song best when firmly tied

to the mast, so stop me if you've heard this one before.
I'm born in the world's figment. Friend of the feather.
I'm trying to stay warm, trying to get this donkey to wear

a hat after it ate my only shrub, and it was a nice one.
A statement followed by a description. The only paradise
is here on earth, although right now it looks like a landfill,

especially after what that zombie dragon did to the wall.
Whose memories are these? I'm trying to make it cohere,
except corduroy is more of a fall fabric and the flowerbeds

aren't speaking to me again, although other creatures
hear them, because fungus is as fungus does. I should read
more fiction, but it all seems that way. At least I've got

a strong online presence, even when my dentist blocked me
after I exclaimed: Don't hate the player; hate the game!
Talk about awkward. Now it's the one big event of the year

as a crowd gathers around the dunk tank during a drought.
With my tax refund I bought a backpack filled with trash bags
to carry toward a new beginning now or later, but the horizon

doesn't extend much beyond the block, with its chronic illness,
its emphysema, its doesn't want to get out of bed. A generator
hums behind the Walmart where skateboarders rarely stick

their tricks, decks clattering across the asphalt like this
while I was out front counting the abandoned cars.
There's no such thing as a clean biscuit or a weapon built

for peace. One sound drowns out another one and so on,
but the light is fading from this world. The Pizza Hut salad bar
ran out of croutons, which makes the teenagers grumpy.

You call it carbo loading; I call it dinner. Yet when it's time
to join the fire brigade, don't worry, I'll be the first one down
the pole. Or maybe the rain will put it out.

PLANETARY LOVE SONG

My stick-figure drawing is quite a likeness
after we slept restlessly all night, mixing
hot and cold, or at least I do, and I'm sorry.
We can visit the disaster without leaving
the house, because it's easier to live together
than it seems, although I guess not you and me.

A fly briefly landed on the windowsill
like a distant cousin or a lunar lander obsessed
with mud before the gaze returns to a face.
A raccoon squeezes through a sewer grate

with its babies nowhere to be seen,
but nature soon returns where humans retreat.

We wear down paving stones with our worry,
like a dog to a pant, pink tongue dangling
over a row of incisors yellowed at the root.
As the music starts up at the bar next door,
tell me, What's the world's smallest turtle?
That's like me to the ocean, you to the sky,

except I can't get this rain out of my head,
or maybe it's the fire sprinklers triggered
by an overloaded outlet at the hospital,
bare feet on the cold tile after the disease
jumped species. Outside the trees begin
to green. We call them buds.

HORIZON LINE

I ate all the cake then sawed away at the remains
      with an inch of leftover floss
            fished from the garbage,
  minty like me in a duckpond
         or catch and release.
Use your hands not your words is the father's law
             pretending to be friendly,
  so let's put some static in here,
           then I'll juggle the next part,
though that won't take the gun away from the police,
    won't break this dollar into change,
  or glue the sky back together
         when you feel alone.

The sale of that hen is paying my expenses;
    otherwise, it's off to the factory
  to build more stuff
      for the landfill or to harvest data.
Farming is hard,
    but so, too, are the speeches.
There's a plague at the heart
     of the kingdom.
Call it medicinal, yet I'm still sick,
      as sorrow thickens around the middle,
This RAV4 won't go any faster,
   its dragging tailpipe making
       a trail of sparks,
    but at least you'll know where to find me,
  and I don't mean under the bed,
      although sometimes there as well.

I dropped my phone in a tray of oatmeal at the truckers' buffet
    because life is a journey
       unless you're stuck,
  then it's more like a grind or a hustle.
There's no turning back from that,
    swapping out the kid's picture pinned to the cubicle wall
  with each new set of school photos
       until the eyelids droop.
   Stick and move.
Even the graveyard has a graveyard,
    and there's a landmark for the massacre,
  but you need to slow down to see it.

It's the domino effect—
     starting with my checkbook.
My computer has a fiercer memory than me,
    as I usually forget
       by the time I reach the bus stop,
    coat wet in the snow.

It should be any minute now,
            although that's what you said
                                    an hour ago.
Clouds fill the window like little feet,
                        because in the end,
        language did it,
                  not you or me.
     I write to try to be free.
The mirror shards me icy,
                        but I can't see across the day.
Everything bends toward a winter sun.

SPECIES

We enter through the front door and leave via the basement,
    the flashlight on my phone illuminating the way
after we wandered into this mess by mistake,
    or maybe it was the result of every choice
we've made—the two often feeling the same.

In other words, no exit, more like a slow road
    to extinction. A deer roamed through the kitchen,
hooves clicking on the tiles. I uploaded the video
    to YouTube where it currently has seven views
plus a stranger trolling me in the comments.

I planned to travel with one carry-on bag, but somehow
    ended up renting a U-Haul and a room full of bees.
I slow-rolled through every stop sign and ended up
    at the dump where I found the texts I sent you
next to a pool of dirty mop water and twisted Kleenex.

The cupboards are empty except for sticky raisins
    and a warm can of Fanta. The car wash for a jumbo jet

must be enormous. It's the art of misdirection
     in an age of surveillance, like taking the h from thong.
Next my head goes over there.

The rest isn't really anyone's business, except for Google,
     Verizon, Facebook, and the NSA. Can I go now?
Notifications off, but I'm still on alert, trying to hang
     a heavy curtain with one arm while a wooden chair
wobbles beneath me. My life. I wish that it was.

BUT IT WON'T STOP THE WAR

I left a yellow bath towel in Baltimore before going over the wall
where I ended up on the outside for less than an afternoon,
then plugged back into the computers on a feeding tube.
I don't remember much else after that, except I'm a renter,
and bargain basement is really neither, more like soda
for the green grocer. That crow is onto my collection of shiny
scraps. Dust to dust. In the Marvel universe, the goal
is retiring to the country, maybe do a little farming.
Mine is the all-you-can-eat buffet or Chicken Little. Just don't
make that pit bull nervous.

The trees talk to each other around the graves. I'm only here
for a moment and trying not to make things worse,
my thumb heavy on the space bar while writing
after visiting hours, yet the words always spill over,
like the crowds that stream out of the movie theater
and into shiny cars in the parking lot dark. You also watched it
on a little screen, a faint glow illuminating your face
as the machines talk to each other without moving their lips,
the land scorched where I thought I might find you
when we are only trying to get to love.

It's quiet enough in the winter, but the damage is still
being done. Some months are harder to pay the heating bill,
and it seems like that and water should be free. Otherwise,
you're on your own with a box of corn flakes and a spatula,
a divining rod and a basket. Just don't make me walk
too far. I'm out of Adderall and easily bored, but Molly sees
the colors in Neapolitan ice cream, while we use napkins
from Arby's to wipe the smear without feeling urgent
because there's a bigger mess behind us and ahead.
We are coming in with the darkest vision.

I'm not making this up. No justice, no peace. We collect
the tweets with the spambots while keeping our eyes
on the mall cop after scooping pennies from the fountain
that you said was for veterans, but I never saw a sign.
Some people read the news and some experience it.
That's not the same as your dream about a leprechaun
on a trampoline. Children sit in detention cells at the border,
while satellites keep track of it all. Life and art are short
as we stand in line for the exit interview with the polar bears
and tree frogs.

The light burned out in the hall, but we had already lost
our way before taking backroads over the mountains
and eating soggy green beans from a can. I agree,
it was weird and awkward like the early stages
of humans and dolphins learning to communicate—
all grunts from us and their playful chirps and whistles.
Maybe that's why this poem is like a paraglider slipping
through the harness. It will do tricks for food,
but has trouble getting out of bed in the morning
after rearranging the furniture in the middle of the night.

The river flows beyond the horizon, and the trash trucks
past that, although they make more of a clank and rumble.
The only people trying to steal your job are the bosses.

No more cookie jar—it's all plastic packaging now. Talk about
lowering the bar. You might as well rest it on the ground
and roll it around with your toe. I would say it was a bad day,
but that implies there are good ones or a set of new jet skis
in the garage when it's more like sink or swim. Feast or famine.
It must have been the leftovers and too much Dramamine.
Frozen flowers means they're not dying.

My condolences to the astronaut who never leaves this planet
because outer space has its own groove. Mine goes
to the back side of Saturn, which is another way of saying,
Please teach me control. I've never made it past the screeners
while listening to Fall Out Boy, I mean, Death Grips, on repeat.
We carry our house in our mouths but it mostly gets stuck
in our teeth, like seeing it through the leaves or behind
the brand name when I'm still in the clink after a dine and dash
without any eating, each nodding head a sunset. I guess
this one will have to do for now.

My key never worked, anyway. I can't seem to remove
this stain from the carpet, but if you stare at it long enough,
it starts to look a little bit like Jesus or Smokey and the Bandit.
That must be why garbage disposals terrify me—something
about them seems slightly alive. Just give me a pill for it after
those body blows or is it the wind beneath my wings,
air horn at the ready for when it's time to slice the pizza
or dragged around at your command, leash chafing the neck
and its IF FOUND, PLEASE CALL tag jingling, then released
into the wild, into the water with the toxins slowly running dry.

First give me a second to send this text. I've always hated
going to sleep, and now the cruise ship horns wake me up early,
or else it's the person shouting the loudest who gets heard,
knuckles wrapping against a plastic helmet that didn't survive
its collision with the concrete. Everything is cracked,
like being pulled underwater while standing on the dock.

A spoonbill dips its beak into the pond and the tadpoles scatter.
Something squishy is stuck to the ceiling, but I'm not going
to touch it. Bottoms up! Chips Ahoy! And maybe for once,
no more dying.

NOT IN SERVICE

I'm grateful for the sun and no hangover,
 for you when you're not in a bad mood,
 for me when I'm not dented and cold.
These people aren't heroes to me.
There's a film over everything
 that connects it
 while rubbing away the rainbow.
It must be all the pharmaceuticals,
 like the slope of a roof we don't notice
 because the body wants to recover,
 but the mind not always so much.

How will we live in this world?
Please chase me around the yard.
We pay for the balloons by letting them go.
A UFO crashed into the hills
 where the ghosts roam
 despite more cars on the road.
Step out of the wreckage.
It's called the glove compartment,
 except that's the last thing
 we put in there, like memory,
 like I'm getting mine.

Party at the firehouse starting now.
Somebody please pick up the phone.
Flies thicken in the heat,

    but nothing can happen
    until mother arrives.
Autobiography is so close to fiction,
    although that doesn't make it
    any less true.
The machines are waiting to take over.
They already know where I live,
    where I sit.

FIRE IN THE HOLE

I tried to leave a message
except the mailbox was full,
probably with all of my other calls,
desperate to order a birdhouse
before they sold out with winter
right around the corner
to bury me or soak
the mattress with fever.

It's hard to steal a dumbwaiter
but not that bike leaning
against the lighthouse.
Time for an upgrade, you said.
Dinner isn't going to make itself,
although I wish it would,
and maybe I should stick
with doing the dishes.

This is like a picture of that,
but not quite. The weight
of tomorrow gets heavier
each day, yet it's better
if you're still here

in the morning,
as dry leaves blow around
right outside my head.

One syllable at a time,
because that's the only sound
that keeps its promise.
Instead, I ate a handful
of raisons and waited
for the lights to turn on
when I'd rather be guilty
of bombing the bass.

If there's a story somewhere,
it's probably about loss,
which can be a form of hope.
The river gets so blue
in the summer, but not
enough to swim in.
That's how it looked online
when counting the pixels.

The continual present
is like a rooster on repeat
grabbing onto the sugars
with fingertips yellow
from cigarettes and Skittles
like a pledge of allegiance
to what defeats us.
I'm only gently steering.

Love is what history can't abide.
Everyone's too busy
to be distracted.
The new gods rapidly age.
I carried the magazine rack

into the bathroom.
What's the point of that?
Exactly.

The houses look as empty
as bank accounts.
The floods dislodge
silver needles from the mud.
But I will miss this Earth
and its playground for squirrels,
its ground for when
you need a rest.

EYES ON THE EXIT

We learn to ride dirty from the castle to the tract house
as a winter sky lowers itself behind the hills.
The mud is just as deep where the ice sheets retreat,
and the penguins are clamoring for a makeover
after chasing a blue butterfly around their bare enclosure,
yet the real lipstick on a pig is the president,
like drip drip drip as the drizzle hits the gutter.

It's gonzo, a world out of control until only the lichen
will survive us and the Spanish Armada, long sunk
beneath the sea, along with the bones this brutal civilization
was built on. In other words, don't say it—spit it,
even if it's all downhill from here, like that go kart
my father pushed me in, no Casper the Friendly Ghost,
just ghosted, and what is wrong with that guy, anyway?

It'll be death by asphyxiation when the last smokestack
blots out the sun, so please pass me a gas mask for now.
Make sure to put it on your own kid first, then get rid of

that fish, since this place stinks enough already, even with
your can of Fresh Start. Mine is called Mildly Horrible,
and together they slept in late while muffins get delivered
to the bakery across the street that doesn't make them.

Although it may have been midwinter's day, that's missing
the bigger picture, such as the stars we place on our tongues.
I'm not writing a memoir erasing the past with the person,
yet sometimes I feel ragged and sad. The cat litter clumps
in the box and on the floor, except that the texts I got
from you were about being sure it was arson or remembering
to take out the trash on Tuesdays. You tell me.

NEXT OF KIN

I locked my keys in the car
        before it rolled across the parking lot
with its bumper sticker that warns
        I BRAKE FOR DAISIES
and a beagle in the back seat.
        Otherwise, it's another wasted day,
a negative keepsake with its opening
        in the shape of a heart.
What time should we go to the party?
I'm leaving soon to get my hair cut,
        so put the fish fillets in the microwave
and the stinger on the bee,
        its bent, thin legs dusted with pollen
and eluding a flock of starlings
        the way I did with those rows of Smirnoff Ice
at the Mini Mart last night.

Let's just say I've moved on.
        Sometimes I even ghost myself.

We're waiting for better weather
        and hoping the check will clear
so that we can eat at Red Lobster
        for your birthday.
We're here to serve, not to rule,
        although I don't know about Mondays.
In any case, you lost me at pop,
        and I don't mean on the press release
or NO DUMPING sign.
        My shopping cart ended up in a ditch
next to the head cleaner
        and I can't make it on my own,
because the spirits still haunt me,
        won't let me sleep.

GRATUITOUS VIOLENCE

No shoes in the house, including that centipede,
because it's getting hot in here,
and the day is full of sneezes
right when somebody stole the last bar of soap
and six of our dishes,
but we eat off of paper plates, anyway,
beneath the forest's tallest tree.

Next on the schedule is a nature hike
where the decorative patterns on our dress
are camouflage against the predators
with their constantly updating financials
and all the money spent on ads
plus a serving of chicken fingers
that aren't fingers and might not even be chicken.

You could say I was out of network,

so maybe we should step into the sunshine,
even though we swallowed the virus—
the one with death swaying
from the fringe on Davy Crockett's jacket.
Language is a carrier of symptoms.
People just want to be free.

The banner should have been placed on the ground
because we didn't see it in the sky.
Sugar is a trigger warning too.
The cheap sunglasses I bought at the rest stop
broke an hour later,
then rested crooked on my nose
for the rest of the drive.

RULES OF THE GAME

Large rigs idle
at a travel plaza,
but don't call it
a comeback,
because we leave
for the desert soon,
except I still
don't know how
we'll get there,
as the countdown echoes
around the launchpad.
The best is getting
lost in reverie
as all the kings fall.
Every brutal settler
carries a dirty bucket
filled with the blood

of tomorrow.
Juice is now
what you smoke,
and the coal plants
are slowly closing.
The various creatures
living in a dead tree
will sometimes try
to eat each other
the way we do.
Satellites beam down
signals to the police.
The next thing
I knew, someone
was yelling, Duck!
We sit in front
of a heater,
but it doesn't
warm us up,
which is the same
as our souls' fate
after driving various
species to extinction.
Then it was time
for a drink.
The law of the father
is brutal,
burning up this
and other worlds,
a plastic spatula
left in the skillet
with a dozen lesions.
A breakfast of Four Loko
is quicker to my ear,
like when you enter

the apartment
while I'm sleeping.
I get lost in a night
that's also time.
Where'd the love go?
Don't worry,
I got this one;
after that,
I'm not sure.
So much
rough draft.

MULTIPLE CHOICE

We see the forest through the living room,
then dump the compost on the floor to let
nature take over. Shadows start their linger
earlier in winter, but I still don't know
where everybody went. Probably avoiding
the hard dinner rolls that supplement our rations.
Yet it wasn't my intention to clear the dance floor,
although it was nice of you to mention gymnastics
when I was mostly flailing around.

I picked up some houseplants along the side
of the road, and maybe a house, too,
after the tangled parachute failed to open,
because the Middles Ages are back again
with everyone struggling to pay the rent
or gathering outside the castle with pitchforks
and torches. It's like what happened to the bees
in synergy with the meadows, their fuzzy little legs
tickling the flowers now gone.

The edge of the world is at my desk.
The bigger thing that we know is coming.
Ghosts speak from across a water shimmering
with the sharp light of stars, as if the other
riverbank is getting closer, although that
might be my mood. Just don't cancel my spot
in the astronaut program—it's so quiet up there
in space minus the static in my headpiece
and the computer always asking to play chess.

The chicken slaughterhouse pays $11.25 an hour.
Squirrels frolic until its dark, then get very still.
When my band played the Viper Room last week,
nobody showed up except Johnny Depp
and a tree pruner. Behind the curtain is madness,
not a doddering wizard, but that's not why
I feel out of sorts. It's because this hat
is flattening my hair after my boss told me
to try using a comb before the meeting.

I mailed a matchbook to a lighthouse and waited
for the downpour before giving myself
the silent treatment for forgetting to pay the vet.
Yet I know there's a new day on the way,
even if it's only another ice age in the morning
because the swelling goes down in the cold.
Anything to keep those needles away from me
when there's so much potential here
once the vampires run out of blood.

Most of the words to this song are Gucci,
so it's easy to sing along. Where there isn't
a cup, we drink from our dirty hands,
then fill up the SUV to drive to the dry cleaners
or into a wall, as I cheer on the late sleepers.
Sometimes the best strategy is to be ineffective

after the goats made short work of the garden
including the straw basket set out for the art
of capture and letting go.

SMOKE AND MIRRORS

I found a friend at Wendy's,
and sometimes we share a meal.
You can serve me with a spoon,
maybe a ladle on a good day,
but then I lost my way.
It wasn't even noon,
and I might not have been awake
when the little man dances in a red suit.
One garbage can for a whole cruise ship.
One ring to rule them all.

It's lovely to feel soft grass beneath
bare feet with toe tips gently tickled.
The wide river is alive
as well as what's inside it.
It was a smooth takeoff
but a bumpy landing
in the gravel pit of our soul
where angels don't fear to tread
and in fact don't tread at all.
Every day I write the book.

It's not the mother of all bombs
but the father of them.
Everything was for sale
until the virus arrived,
then everything was for the wiping.
I don't know where the time went

or why the sun dropped out of the sky.
It must have been the special effects,
although that doesn't make
these tears less real.

EASY MONEY

The message never got delivered
    after the skywriter ran out of gas
as beachgoers dive for cover
    at the D-Day reenactment.

The light takes longer to reach me
    and the fireman with emphysema.
Both of us have bills to pay,
    as freight trains rumble in the distance.

Cows stand in their own manure
    so that we can tug on their udders,
but the machines don't drink milk,
    while we caress the polished gleam.

Despite these many words, the mystery
    of the missing leftovers remained intact.
Mochi or mocha or gnocchi—
    some language is meant for licking.

A yellow bulb shines in a distant window,
    as screens glow blue in the darkness.
We move through empty streets,
    rain muffling the night in our voices.

Then the landlords return with a vengeance
    like a syntax coming back

to punish me for my distractions
    and tube socks drying in the tub.

I'm trying to loosen the leash
    with its dog tags etched in metal
because we will give it all away
    before they come to take it.

TAKE IT OR LEAVE IT

The whole town turned out for the parade,
    but it was the wrong day,
                or at least
that's what the police said,
        and right now
    they're the ones with the guns.
There's a leak in the ceiling which means
    more time down here
             cleaning up the mess.
That's different from minor home repairs
    conducted while drunk.
Those always end up
        a little bit crooked,
    like the stitching
        on Fred Flintstone's pelt.
The afternoon feels longer in the clinch
    while quietly eating a sandwich
              at my cubicle
    and watching YouTube on mute.
It's a long drive to the sea,
        especially on the back roads,
    from anarchists to zookeepers.
I've started writing for the machines.

It's raining and sunny at the same time,
    which is closer to a hot mess
            than a poetics.
Water drips from the broad green leaves
    while we get eaten
        by the corn.
You called it clickbait,
        although it might be
    a gothier version.
Bluebird   Hummingbird   SUV
My head went over there
        with the tangle
            of electrical cords
    in another dumb conundrum,
so I swung a wrecking ball through it,
        and now I can no longer
            find you
    after retrieving all the shopping carts
        from the parking lot.
History never stops for the dispossessed.
            The imagined can be just as real.

HOLES IN THE SURFACE

Please don't let the silence
    overtake me.
I only have a few things
    to say.
They don't include instructions
    on how to use
the new gas grill
    which the fire department
has already extinguished
    a couple of times.

I can't help it that I'm partial
        to lighter fluid.
The end will come
        soon enough,
so the question is what gets
        left behind.
Maybe a landfill
        turned into a public park.
Maybe a song
        to hum.
All these strands of light.

BEGIN AGAIN

I can't remember what we spent our money on
or how the known became a commercial,
as vampires chew the scenery with the ground
too cold to dig a hole. Wind and water caused most
of the erosion along with a heavy wheelbarrow
we used to move a tattered couch across the yard
where a dog barks whenever its owner is away,
its water bowl tipped over in a dandelion patch.
Blue jays and squirrels battle at an empty feeder,
while clouds of hazy smoke fill the valley
and the bulldozers wait for us to leave.

After tonight, the season changes again, finds me
under the covers with a slice of sponge cake
while outside a Yankee Clipper gets wedged
in harbor ice, its thick timbers splintering
and stars gleaming like rhinestones in the sails.
How often does a wolf go hungry? I wait
for a knock at the door, but I'm afraid the repairs
will never be completed, which isn't the same

as adjusting the meds or when the caribou migrate
the wrong way with smaller trails leading off from
the main one while predators keep a quiet watch.

Groups of retirees exercise at a shuttered mall,
brisk-walking around broken glass and slushie stains.
From end to end eight times makes a mile,
except that I'm wayward, I'm all over the place,
and that will be the legacy for now. Yours got eaten
by moths on the estate and its collection of dents.
More sunsets. People are getting desperate.
In the winter we can see the sky through the trees
when the only thing I have left is a crispy Yule log
and the kind of drumsticks you can't eat
when I'd rather go crazy shaking my tambourine.

So much can happen in those magical moments.
According to the youth group named The Little Alpines,
the zoo hippo climbed a snowdrift out of its enclosure
unlike whatever it is scratching around in the attic,
tuning fork at the ready for when we next crater.
We had an hour to kill before our train arrived,
although you wouldn't know it from the metronome.
Every table had already been taken, so we ate
outside by the curb where the long view
briefly came into focus, your night-vision goggles
pushed to the top of your head.

Are we there yet? Children put wheels on a soapbox
and roll it to the orphanage. My kingdom
for a compost heap. My kingdom for a quatrain.
We'll know when we reach the end of the world,
but there will still be something for sale and a satellite
burning up as it plunges back to earth. To be honest,
I don't really feel like it. Like a broom this poem
has a certain sweep and may eventually need

a breath mint. Next you'll be telling me that the wind
is windy, that corn is easy to digest. My progeny
is a bell tower, though I've been on my own for a while.

It might feel impossible to continue, but my Corolla
still makes the commute to Cleveland, although
I sometimes have trouble staying between the lines,
so I'll sing this one loudly while it brings me joy
like karaoke with ghosts and I'm always out of tune,
then pull the portable heater in close with a lone Cheeto.
It's also where a forest appears in our dreams
as the sun glows inside the leaves, the clouds striated
with purple, pink, and peach. Keep on shining.
You've got more technology than me, so go ahead
and plug me in. The alarm lights up every time it rings.

Eggs tumble down a conveyor belt beneath carcasses
swinging from hooks. Some are whispered to slaughter
and some are driven. A fence blows over in a storm.
I want to live in a different world, which is why
we're always getting ready to go, or maybe we mean
on the verge of leaving. It's the duck-and-cover bucket
we fill up during active shooter drills, so what
should I do with all of this glue when history sticks
to us? First comes ragged, then comes unraveling.
That was before I checked my latest texts, wondering
what happened to the rest of the words.

DRIFTING TO STARLIGHT

Ambient noise is the chainsaw or hair dryer,
maybe a garden gnome rustling a bush.

Raid® kills bugs dead, except for that one,
as the pile of dirty laundry grows.

I watched a screen through another screen.
We sunk a paddleboat with the butt of a musket.

No set of wings will keep this body aloft for long,
yet I'll still hum a tune from the belly.

The city's concrete absorbs the summer heat,
as does the cooler filled with warm sodas.

An animatronic trout twitches on its mount.
There's lead in the baby food and water.

Pain radiates outward, however small the spot.
The spaces in between are filled with profit.

You're welcome to wrestle this mop from my hands,
just as long as you give me back my poodle.

This here and now is nothing but trouble.
Memory surfaces when it smells blood.

My dummy in a landslide. My canceled flight.
All these roads lead away from home.

GO LONG

I'm only here for the free beer
and maybe the bean dip.
Everything else is for sale
including this neck splint
and tire-pressure gauge,

this single-serving packet
of dehydrated saliva.
The terror might be building,
yet the brutality
was always there,
much longer for sure
than the Taco Bell Gorditas
we accidentally left
in the back seat
during a heat wave
after we got our
one hour of freedom,
sometimes per day,
sometimes per week,
and far away
from the throne room.
Otherwise, all we know
is what's been lost—
a million species extinct
and part of a weave
slowly filling with stone.
I'll drown holding onto it
and only float
when my body starts rotting.
Heavy is the try,
says Yoda, and sighs,
or maybe I'm misquoting,
although it wouldn't be
the first time.

Dead bees everywhere.
A scarecrow leans
in a fallow field.
The last time I checked,
the light was slowly fading
and the trucks were driving fast,

stirring up a cloud of husks
obscuring a view to the sea
and its floating Ferris wheel
rotating through sharks
and a coral reef,
through a gurgling oil spill.
So much dinghy,
so little time
as the children come out to play
with a future melted
like a clown's makeup
after a long day making
animal balloons in the sun,
red smeared across the mouth
and back of the hand,
a bit how Robert Smith
applies lipstick.
Yet once the oceans warm
it's all over,
as the jellyfish plot
their dominion,
their bigger sticky,
like me and the cinnamon bun
someone left next to
the food court garbage can,
its glazed raisins embedded
in random patterns
the way I've been known
to take a lil' nibble.

I'm trying to do this without
looking at my phone,
but it keeps blowing up.
Pour the grease into
the coffee can by the sink.
I'm the kind of cook

who scorches the Teflon.
We tried to stop the violence,
but it was everywhere.
The squirrels in the yard
were oblivious to it all
except for changes
in their terrain such as
predators and the weather—
kind of like us, in fact.
I don't know
where else to go.
I can't land on a lake
the way the flock does;
instead, I'll keeping trying
to hiccough time.
We trade Tide for Oxy
and Oxy for a TV
until the widow stole it back.
In Pittsburgh they used
whiskey for currency.
Me? I'll stick with toothpaste
applied with my finger
after that last trip to the dentist
scraping beneath the gum line.
You called it a deep cleaning;
I called it bleeding,
just as some days are better
than others.

At least the last leaves
haven't fallen,
although they will soon,
white tips of a mockingbird's wings
flashing through the trees
the way memories return.
The past is either a reverie

or a nightmare
as the fire siren echoes
in a valley preparing for winter.
So do you with soup.
I laughed and I cried,
but there was little in between.
Right now I'm more
on the sadness side.
Yesterday too.
The day before that
I shared some funny memes.
Just don't take me
to your leader—
things are already
fucked up enough.
A thousand points of light,
and most of them
on their knees.
More music, less talk.
Same gatekeepers, different locks.
We take the long route around,
tugging a droopy kite
as a chipmunk scampers
across the path
or maybe it was the mouse
I saw in 7-Eleven
pondering its options.

Over the course of an afternoon
we moved the woodpile thirty feet
only to watch it
go up in flames
after dousing it with kerosene
because, as you said,
it was something to do.
Shadows move quickly

around the human
while satellites orbit the Earth,
sending messages directly
to the headphones tight
over our ears and jaw
until the world starts to ache
when we visit
the animal shelter for life.
How did doo-doo get
on the window viewing
a sidewalk lined with
flapping miniature flags
stuck in Easter baskets
and assorted jellybeans?
Bunny has gone to ruin.
There's a big wave crashing
on top of us,
and this poem is a scooter
working its way
down the page
while you're at Zumba,
each word spinning
its own set of wheels
or else it's a delivery van
crashing through the store's
front window.

For exercise I walked
around the block,
then had to stop for ice cream
after Baskin-Robbins advertised
a sale on sundaes.
I think food may be a metaphor,
but I can't stop the feed
or fill these empty spaces,
although this evergreen-

scented candle helps
like the transistor radio
I listened to while calling
all the bars in town
to find you.
The American night
is also its day.
Children sleep on concrete floors
in containment camps
at the border of a land
swept with genocide
in a hurricane of knives.
Bring the noise.
Then bring it again.
This is my story,
but I can't get there from here
although I know the way
along with where
they keep the money.
We'll kiss and tell
at the wishing well
or at least at our hotel
out by the airport
with something absolutely still
beneath the bed.

The wind blew the clouds away
including the pot smoke
leaking through a sunroof
and the echoes of
"Born in the USA" on repeat
while a car idles
in the hospital parking lot
before we visit
grandpa on a gurney,
Dr. Phil muted

on the waiting room TV,
or maybe it was at the laundromat
where I'll be later
because fluffing is
part of the process.
I'm not talking about
my sunnier disposition
when I get off of work
or how it can be difficult
to know when someone
is crying in the rain.
Just ask that cyborg
or the swaying trees.
Yet nature always gets
its revenge,
which is why I saved
the soggy biscuits
along with your old mittens.
Time squeezes us all,
but that won't stop us
from talking through the movie
starring gas stations and beer,
but maybe not
in that order.

We thought the police
couldn't see us,
but we were like fish fillets
in Saran Wrap—
and just as clingy.
There's a lot of anxiety
at the mall.
I'm going to live off of
the royalties from this song,
then study the history of fungus
beginning with a corner

of the shower.
When objects touch each other
they create a little magic,
although a therapist
can explain it better
since I'm from out of state,
and it can be difficult to let go
of the hurt.
A dog chases a cat
like a worry.
The only things free to stream
are *Kung Fu Panda 2*
and the latest installment
of *Shark Week*.
I called it alone time,
but it lasted
a whole life,
as teenagers aimlessly wander
the street like zombies
consuming sugary drinks
instead of brains
and returning to Pizza Grill
for free refills.

The night turns outward.
The fireworks are louder
than bright.
When you say goat
do you mean
the greatest of all time
or the animal
that eats feces?
I'm fine with either.
I had to wait to get paid
before writing the rent check,
even if I keep learning

that everything goes away
in the end,
except for this office job.
At least I got a chair
that swivels
and a spot near the bathroom
so that I can jiggle
the handle whenever
the toilet runs.
Where did I go when I left?
Seems like kind of nowhere.
The horizon got closer
at the shooting range
where we fire into
the belly of God
sagging over the pasture
as migrating geese
make November V's
following a river below
until it reaches the bay
where the container ships
wait in formation.

I went to see *Cats*
and the cast
wouldn't stop singing.
Better that, I guess,
than cabin fever,
hungry for a fix,
curtains drawn
and the damage done.
A thick filament.
Faint light.
My precipice.
It is the hardest thing
to get free.

There are so many dreams
we missed,
yet you can never
go home again,
so send in the clowns
or the taco truck,
create a new community.
How much is this parakeet
going to cost me in seeds?
I'd prefer to hear
the snow leopard purr.
My heart aches,
but my head aches worse
watching all of this
destruction unfold
along with whatever
mystery ingredient you added
to the potato salad
before we loosened the belt
and sold the rented Bentley
for scraps.

The blind bird watcher
identifies each one by song
while lying in a recliner
while I build my Tower of Babel
otherwise known as walk it
like I talk it
or maybe hop along.
I haven't been cleared
for takeoff yet.
Instead, the messages
get delivered by dictation.
The cut is cleaner
than it looks,
but I've got a thing about dirty

and slouching in the lineup.
Here we go again.
A cold front
dipped into Florida,
into the gravy boat.
The banks say borrowing,
but it feels like
stealing to me.
I bought a sequined top
at Old Navy after folding
endless piles of clothes.
I'm seasonal,
so I can wear it
to the slopes or beach
like a baby shark stopper
splashing in the shoals
or brush the polyester
until it tingles,
static rippling the surface,
hair pulled up tight in a bun.

Remove the candy bar
from the wrapper,
the ladle from the stream,
which is also time,
and time is death.
Would you believe it?
We have doom on the phone.
It's dark already,
but the children
don't seem to notice
while I wait
for a knock at the door
from the arsonist
asking for a glass of water,
and then pretend

I'm not around,
always the bridegroom,
never the bride.
In the meantime,
get me out of here
with the rest of the pedestrians.
The tooth fairy sneezed on me,
so I know it's real,
yet Santa wants
to come down the chimney
then leave me in the lurch
when I write him
after the holidays.
It's quietest beneath
a blanket of snow
and the lights off
in all the houses.
Too bad the law
is always so noisy.

Don't give me the leash
or a helmet for the crash course,
dummies inflating around me
as metal crumples
against the wall.
I keep Q-tips under the sink,
but I won't stick them
in my ear like a rotisserie
or consider it the good life
as the juices collect
in the foil pan
along with the heads
in Sleepy Hollow.
I can't help it.
This is my story.
Still life with can opener

and opposable thumb
or else you can try
to pry the lid loose
with a screwdriver and hammer.
Later, we used the can
as a vase for stubby daisies,
then wondered how we'll pay
for the heat this winter,
although you might also say
it's getting hot in here.
Humans will hunt
anything to extinction,
including its own.
The Weed King lords over
a ruined garden
with an ambulance
resting on cinderblocks out back,
its steering wheel missing.

Wind billows the trees and curtains.
Are we at the end already?
The soul peels from the body
like a wrapper to candy
or a raccoon to the trash
as wolves howl in the city,
but first I need to finish
these three loads of laundry
gathered from the floor.
This cold has turned me
into an atrocious nose blower
posting new photos
to an Instagram account
featuring groomed poodles
of the Cosa Nostra.
I can't compete.
It's the war

of all against all,
and only carnivores nap;
the rest are on the run
as a police cruiser
pulls into the driveway,
its siren a different song.
We build a small fire inside
with these notes
toward a kindling.
Groove is in the heart
and maybe somewhere else.
There's more than enough
for everyone.
Small cone of light.
Blue heron on a far shore.
Sound might make it go,
but baby says boom.

ROUNDING THE CORNER

Snow collects where we stepped
    except for when you carried me
       to the kennel.
You might say I had two desserts.
The correct answer is total disaster
    or emo trampoline.
We take medicine to fix it
    by ourselves.
All that dust comes from the grave,
    grass growing
    through the mouth.
It makes sense that it would be about escape.

I can see for miles in the night,
    which makes me the opposite
    of a bat.
That's a long way to go for a drink,
    and where are the song birds now?
Down in Pensacola.
The park is next to the lake,
    along with the family reunion,
    like finding Nemo except worse.
Either way, we probably won't get paid,
    with this bowl made of spills
    and a fist in it.

I didn't have far to go before toppling over.
It may have been gravity
    or my kindergarten teacher.
I adjusted the flue so that it's not so smoky
    after you built a fire
    to chase away the cold.
The darkness encroaches,
    is so much larger than us.
Small balls of fuzz collect on a green sweater.
The sky is a screen filled with sparrows
    that form notes
    a rifle plays.

I would write this from beginning to end,
    but life keeps getting
    in the way.
A shark screams through the steel,
    as my head snaps back
    at the violence.
That blackhole has a lifetime appointment.
Yet if you wind me up I'll sing,

    like the plastic monkey
    on the mantle.
Pirates at sea are pirates at play.
Each letter is a little drawing.

BUTTERFLY ON THE BREEZE

The sign painter fell down
and won't be getting up
after putting sense in a trash can,
then banged on the lid for rhythm.
At least that's how it feels on a Monday
as a stunt jumper takes out
a herd of sheep in the Hebrides
to the low moan of a foghorn—
but don't worry,
I'm still going to get mine.

Why do the administrators get paid
the most around here?
Boots, meet Burger King.
Sneeze, meet sleeve.
We'd rather say metaphor,
except we can't when everything
is so carefully managed
even if the baskets have leaks,
and we know where the bodies are.

We put chips in the crockery
after waking up late,
take a halberd to the tent pole.
I'm in the system,
like a gallop that's all legs

and the red blood drying brown.
Tear the flag from the mast.
Collect the birds.
When I blow on the whistle,
it's just full of spit.

BREAKING NEWS

I promise this one will make more sense
just as soon as I get paid,
but I'm going to need a little more focus
and less talking to the surgeon.
Humble beginnings.
                        Humble endings.
Yet we still managed to go off the rails.
At this rate, we'll be lucky if we break even
or have time to type up our report
about the crossing guards with their guns drawn.
This place is kind of crazy.
Monkeys squat in the sun.

We take Adderall until our hands shake,
although I don't recommend it.
Animals move into the abandoned factory.
The dairy farms are deep in debt.
The darkness beckons
                       as much as the light.
The line at the grocery store at night
is mostly older men buying pudding and beer.
Everyone wanted to kiss the baby at the christening.
I wish I wouldn't obsess about your leaving.
We paint right over the holes with our rollers,
singing, Let the music play.

The weather warmed up in time for the funeral.
I liked it better when we didn't have to buy stuff.
We spent the afternoon with our mothers.
It's midweek, and already the laundry bag is full.
This empire will eventually fall,
                                      and the one after that.
There are more and more people shouting,
as if all we ever do is listen for announcements.
We dig out after another storm.
Whatever dislodges the crown.
Maybe we don't want to be found.

NEON CATASTROPHE

I fell in a hole while staring at my phone,
           but the pratfalls started long before that.
The machines know more about us than we do,
           so watch me pose with this plug,
    with my supply of donuts and metalworking,
           of bird cages and childcare,
or a pain that almost went away
           until we gather it back up again
    like a need that never left us
           or a nurse commuting to work on a treadmill.

Mourning doves sing their sweet solace
           from a nearby tree.
That might be hard to reproduce
           with a stick-and-poke tattoo—
    maybe we should try a sun or daisy.
You can also just hope for the best
    as I scrub this pile of dishes
           while wearing a thick chain connecting

     my wallet to my belt
because you stole more than my heart and my car.

We tune out the noise to hear the static.
I've got blue on repeat where the contrails
    spell out my name in fading letters.
My space heater is in the repair shop
    where I saw someone attach it to a lathe,
  but I'm an amateur all the way,
    so what do I know?
I got cold cleaning out the basement
    and waiting for your texts.

The ribbon on my lapel is mostly for show,
    although I remember it being pinned to me
  at the end of a long night out.
I'm trying to find the light switch
    or maybe just the light.
Google maps the war as it increases,
    but it will never locate every star.
The duck form is a lot of squat,
    as we move the words around like furniture
  or watch otters glide through a kelp bed.

I used to be dip and dive like that;
    now I'm doodle on a loop and clipping coupons
  while waiting for the sea water
    to come over the wall
  and float the picnic table into the bay.
The barcode can be applied as a sticker.
Wrinkled candy wrappers blow around in my head.
  Sometimes you have to let it go.
No more plastic inside the whale's stomach.
No more of so many things.

COMING TO AMERICA

I saw the land and then it vanished in a fog
of history and war as the words warp
in the middle and also around the edges
as if the forest were only there to drive through
or we took our show on the road without
ever standing up. That was before I spent
most of my money on a bad haircut
and the rest on a slot machine to practice
for my trip to Las Vegas and health care.

The high school bleachers emptied out
after the game while clouds of pale moths
swarm the stadium lights and tire treads
flatten patches of grass. Mostly we're buying
time, but the costs are extinction.
Meth makes the edges hard and cold,
and this cinnamon gum is starting to lose
its flavor, but in the rich man's house
I don't have anywhere else to spit it.

Some said it was the best hoagie in Philly,
but I only licked the wrapper, then pulled
my chair up close to the screen. The cling
is a rush of dopamine as the sun shines down
on the bodies or we sleep in our car
by the airport, although it's not as if
we've got anywhere to go with a pocket full
of loose change and miniature Snickers.
That one makes me sick.

The sky widens where it clears as geese
migrate along its periphery and the road
bumps into a mountain: the road
is called vision and the mountain is a grave.

We leave the best part to the snow,
then build a temporary shelter in the desert
where swallows nest in the eaves, or maybe
they're bats—it's hard to tell in the darkness,
which makes other things so clear.

The heart won't open without the lungs.
The lungs won't open without the breath.
The dog sheds all over the furniture,
and so do we. Everywhere I look, I find
our remains. The earth is thick with what's
come before, frequently with a blade or bullet
lodged in it. During an ice age, it's not
the freeze that kills you when the executioners
are usually hiding in plain sight.

The wheel spins in place until it becomes the place,
yet the hole keeps getting deeper until water
begins to fill it making my bottom muddy,
my cochlea gummed. And sometimes the wheel
won't go or goes so slow. At least that's what
the pharmacist told me while stuck in Chicago
during the fireworks. The prescription left
my liver intact but not my wallet or the RV's
mini-fridge wedged beneath the windshield.

Thunder rumbles in the distance to the tune
of here it comes. But don't worry. I'm holding on
for now. I've got hope. And biscuits, although
nothing to dunk them in except an oil spill.
It is happening again. It's always the fall
of America. It's like clicking on a link inside
your head, although that won't fix this toothache
after my dentist canceled my appointment
because I couldn't stop chattering.

There's meat for Easter. We might win
for the most diversions, the most unnecessary
bathroom breaks at work. Tell me more while
we rubberneck from our seats. It's Ernest
with an "a," not the one who went to camp
during a summer so still it became its own shadow
before shaking like a Chihuahua at the liquor store.
That's bad behavior, but I can relate
after giving away most of my information.

We have squandered an abundance and known
indiscriminate slaughter. Sound and light
filter through glass forming a panorama
of genocide and enslavement. Even the children
can't talk freely, live in fear of their parents' rage,
as a train speeds through the night in our dreams.
Cash and carry. Guns and ammo. Porn.
A roadside shrine marks the spot of the crash.
I almost made it.

There's a competition at the fire station
to see who can own the biggest pickup truck,
but you've got to be a bit fearless to run
into the flames, to take these broken wings.
Musicals scrub history of its disease,
but I'm not pumice. Instead, I got down
on my knees and smoothed the dirt
with my hands. Bees love other bees.
The body at rest is still fitful.

DIFFERENCE IN THE SAME

The executioner's gut eclipses his belt
whether he stands up or bends over.
I would sell ads on my YouTube channel
except it doesn't get any views.
I guess no one wants to watch me
blow up an inflatable pool,
but I also love poetry for what it can't do.

The seminarian's dream isn't a meat pie.
The next step is to give it all away,
yet I'll bet you $100 that squirrel finds its nut
alongside these words buried in a field.
My neck itches, and it's called shingles
or a chafed wattle. Nothing stays unchanged,
including winter's steel creep.

I hear sex through the floor and yelling
through the walls, and sometimes vice versa,
but there's only silence at the lake
except when it gurgles. On certain nights
I sleep at the bottom of it, like a dirty hand
in a dirty glove, while the trees
are always talking along its blue shore.

I ate an egg sandwich in Memphis
after getting poked in the eye, so I wear
my sunglasses at night, yet the trouble
is larger than me as the letters
arrive in a rush and a jumble. It is the end
of fear but not of heartache, but at least
I can put away this cardboard apron.

Now I'm free to wander the matrix
where our snow angels mix with ash.

No two are the same and love is
in the difference, although there aren't enough
tears to grieve for what's also been done
in its name. A bare message, no envelope;
head cracked open.

CAPTURE THE FLAG

Thistle is a spice to the raptor trying to
                                        escape this island
              along with us.
You declared it springtime as the snow fell,
       though it kept us warm waiting in line
             for the latest upgrade.
Call me old-fashioned,
                    but I already have my implant,
and I've given a thousand baskets to the Easter Bunny
      or the equivalent of one
                        for each egg this poem laid.

Don't forget the tears I shed at the movies,
      because if that's the carrot,
              then I'd hate to see the stick.
Yes, but how does that make you feel?
Like a speck in the universe,
                    except then it's easier
      to slip between grooves in the tread.
Plus, this belt has room to expand
                          like a neck trap hidden
         deep in the forest.

He was always going to leave,
                and so was she,
          until there's no difference between

                    being compelled and being summoned—
just ask the competitive eaters.
I was a late addition to the lineup,
                    although I play
     a variety of positions
              such as chipping the glaze.

Other designs can be found on Tumblr
                        with crocheted antlers
    as I sort through the lost and found
       after you gave the artistry
                        a gentle spanking.
The long-suffering wife would be putting it mildly.
The world is on fire and getting warmer,
     so never leave a stove unattended,
and keep the candy corn away from where
                     the lungs hurt.

FULL DISCLOSURE

The valet drove away with all the cars
but left us the spaceship.
We think about what can't be defeated
while there's so much else to lose,
starting with this heartache.
In horror films, sometimes the threat
comes from within the house
and sometimes from without.
That's how I found the ghost in me,
and it didn't take much sleuthing,
like a bear to the camping site cooler.

What's a lumberjack without a saw?
What's a poet without a helmet?

I save the receipts for everything
except Twizzlers.
You nodded and filled your pocket
with old tissues and sugar cubes,
with every quiet passing,
like the time you said
we needed to make some cuts,
and I was happy to be one of them
because this place is starting to suck.

I used to have the phone number for NASA.
Now there's a constant ringing
in the ears after a drone strike
took out the lemonade stand.
I'm saving my best dress shirt for heaven.
The apex predator is the sun.
When we light every scented candle,
it smells a bit like gasoline
with a vague hint of citrus.
I know this from my math class
and the fire drill in my head.

My potential is two liters of Mountain Dew,
except that I've had another setback.
When an orca hunts a shark,
it goes straight for the liver,
but my father's would have gotten it drunk.
The only thing I would repeat
is that we're running out of time.
That's a lot of scraps for the compost—
green like every can of peas,
like a mound of moldy cheddar,
then stir it for the bacteria swarm.

How did we get there from here?
I blame it on amnesia

during lifeguard training.
History is so much bigger than this.
Saints silently slip away
after somebody called the police,
as the orders come from above
where Santa once flew—
just ask the flock of birds
that always returns to the same tree,
hollow in winter.

ENOUGH SAID

Bees will make a nest in the mouth
of almost anything dead.
I'd prefer paradise be here on earth.
I peeked underneath a cricket
and saw an entire world.
The sky spread forever from there.
My letter. My song quality.
My let this one slip away.

DEEP SHINE

The highway markers tick by like a clock or years at sea
as we squeeze more fun from the book of love,
then get a speeding ticket after being rear-ended.
Hopefully, the storm is mostly over,
so let me know when you're coming through.
I've got paper plates and most of my molars,
yet I don't remember anything about a wedding.
I was only trying to catch a little sun behind the Walmart,
but instead was hungover the next day.

Serves me right, you said, for going down with a ship
called the Rum Boat.

Maybe that's why there seems to be a cooling trend
occurring right here at home
where a sullen toad squats in my skull.
The next thing I knew you were texting me from the vet,
as my information is continually hoovered,
phone vibrating on the kitchen counter.
The shortcut to the toilet goes through my room
where a weathervane gets the bed spins
like Baby Yoda in his floating stroller.
What exactly is that guy's point, anyway?
Take something. Do something to it. Do something to that.

There was also the time I stole the dog bowl,
which feels a bit like starting at the bottom,
but now the whole team's here.
Or we could make an egg house with the ones
those chickens are always laying.
I'm sick of it is the only way I can say it and not spit it.
Somehow, I've almost filled up this page,
although the damage was done a long time ago,
loving too much or too little the way a cat does,
but who doesn't enjoy getting rubbed beneath the collar?
Let's imagine what we're capable of.

TANGLE OF WISHES

KINDRED SPIRITS

Most of speech is a lie,
so call me the lil' dribbler.
Amateur astronomers discovered a black hole
right there in the middle of summer.
Bean sprouts grow around it,
along with a case of beer.
We found some of it for sale at the drugstore,
but didn't want to upset the stroller
parked next to the sliding doors.

There's a bend in the river
every time I come to visit.
Maybe I should work late today.
This train platform will be cold in winter.
Regardless, it'll need to get darker
before we can show that film.
I can sit still for this
until I'm trademarked by Nabisco
or just pretend to act moody.

A slowly spinning carousel
twinkles brightly in the forest.
Hunters wear an orange vest over camo.
We don't check the mail
as much as we used to.
For day trips, it's good to pack a lunch.
Resignation isn't always a form of defeat.
Miners carry their own air into the mix
of dust and glitter.

DIRTY VINYL. JUICY FRUIT.

I spent all my days on what won't move,
then lost my hat beneath a glacier.
You said it was a notepad.
Money talks louder than me, even in disguise.
I got confused by early dismissal.
My doctor prescribed a pill,
but I'd rather salvage the deep fryer.
There's a shape to what falls
between the cracks. There's a shape
to every ruin, including this gift basket
three weeks later.

We traded it in for amusement-park tokens
that I can't use any faster on the log ride.
The flight schedule is a diversion.
We ransack the laundry for ready-to-wear.
The latest collection features
two buns per patty or a bolero tight
against acid reflux. I need time off
from the light bent by a snow globe.
The ice isn't thick enough for skating.

We spent the rest of winter on the run,
yet couldn't avoid the traffic
after stopping to tug on the Dairy Queen levers
we found behind Touchdown Jesus.
Does dystopia have a diphthong?
I can barely carry a tune.
In the land of a thousand lakes,
some of them must be puddles.
They come free with my address book
and yours,
                    sincerely

THE WAR AT HOME

You might be an heir to the throne,
but I've abolished the monarchy
before the sun comes out
and washes away the DayGlo.
That doesn't mean I'm going to hold
a parade for Oxycontin.
Besides, you meet all kinds
of interesting people in hotel bars.
This one has a little dance floor
which lights up in the dark.

A car wreck at the garden party
scattered the caterers
though not the guests.
Children swam unattended in the pool.
A small dog ran to where
the clam chowder spilled.
I posted a photo, but no one liked it.
Later, I got an online ad
for a leash and mucus reducer,
yet my banking app takes me
straight to porn.

I should probably tell someone,
except they already know.
What are visiting hours
with the mentally ill?
Diamond cutters drown out
the bustle of no beaches,
only parking lots and a large lawn
for feeding squirrels
in front of the courthouse.
The few items I'd rescue from a fire

fit in a plastic bag destined
for recycling or a landfill.

A vaporizer isn't a sci-fi weapon—
it's used for getting high.
Fluffer designates a range of roles,
just as I've watched the police
invent the law on the spot.
We get time off for good behavior
the way camo matches the couch
or lessons are fitted to the student.
That didn't keep us from later
losing our tools in the lake.

The only heaven is here on earth,
even if I'm always waking up
with a head full of fumes.
It's what I get for living so close
to the highway, because you
never know when it's time to go.
So take down the flag.
Take the medals off the table.
Pine boxes come in various sizes,
and carry their song inside.

SELFIE IN A CONVEX MIRROR

1)
It was warm in the sun, but I'm not a lizard
humming winter like a jingle. Instead, we slip
the dishes in bubble wrap and suck
from the rotisserie, asking *Are those jeggings?*
while ducking a drunken roundhouse.

The NSA is now spying for the banks,
but they won't find my collection of melted
candy bars hidden beneath the mattress.
I'm saving them to use as sticky paddles
when the icecaps melt or as gold medals
awarded at the mental velodrome in Atlantis.
In other words, we're doomed,
but I hold out hope for creative solutions.
I'm going under, nose plugs at the ready after
misplacing the car keys and photobombing
the panda bear webcam. Collapsing new buildings
is one translation, though you gotta have friends
before you can have frenemies, the cutthroat
bingo players with a single number on their cards
as azalea bushes blaze sapphire blue outside
the cafeteria. I stuck my whole head in them,
and then in your book about linens,
which includes a special section on the rags
used to wipe down deli counters.
Talk about visceral, except I got a tattoo
on my inner ear and the only word I can hear
is jackhammer, even if a story isn't always
in the telling. Besides, how much
is there really to say about a new puppy?
I wrote this poem on my phone before throwing it
in the toilet, but my head hurts too much
to do the math. This isn't a footnote—
it's a leather machine, kinda punky
with ripped spandex and smelling of Jergens.
Yet eventually the creatures close in.

2)
We rattle the locks on the door and bring
the sergeant to his knees, saluting
the ultimate viscosity of it all on his way down.

The luckier ones get to sneak in a pirouette
or field fungos while a marching band
tramples the grass and moves the goal posts
whenever we're not looking. I could take a pill
for that, cry out to the dark lake with its crackling
along the wire, or a skip-it J.Crew filibuster
that leaves a dent on the tray table jostling
my ribcage, on the trash my mom washes.
No wonder I'm terrified of the oral surgeon
and the stockboys taking their talents
to the stockyards downwind from school.
I set off the fire alarm every time I cook,
watching the luggage tossed into the ship's wake,
saying I'm so outta here, or maybe just distracted
for a minute, because the only life to love
is this one. Yet sometimes things end badly
and never get repaired; this poem is one example.
Thank god, though, for Dunkin' Donuts,
where my wife works. There's a difference
between nonlinear and simply scattered.
I whacked at it for a while with a fish head,
meat still sticking to the bones until
we removed it with our fingers as street sweepers
very slowly trail the last marathoner to finish.
You could call the self-portrait a series
of minor abrasions. Or you could read it
without a mic. And by dog, you could be referring
to a person. The house is set off from a road
being swallowed by the desert
as the afternoon light shines more sideways,
like a constriction in the throat of the sky,
even though it's our turn to speak.

BORROWED TIME

I eat rice pudding for dinner
and listen to a report about
today's mass shooting.
The biggest feed lots
are visible from the moon,
along with a plastic palm tree
shoved into the corner.
I carry you and your
backpack, although
you're the one who sets
me down, as I always
had trouble letting go.

So where's the narrative?
Lost at sea with the rest
of the crew busily
constructing a new one.
I take the wound
to the suture, though not
what comes next,
since we'll all be working
until we're eighty, anyway,
while the boss lives at home
with anger management issues
and imminent winter.

THE DARK NET

1)
We took a dozen quizzes and failed every one,
but I know I'm gonna ace this next personality test.
You'd think that might get me far in this job,

except I didn't go to the right college,
and now I'm just another parent getting drunk
on cheap margaritas at Chuck E. Cheese's
while the kids do whatever.
These are the final days, and I don't care.
Turns out the fire started inside the house.
Maybe that's how me, my ex-,
and my ex-'s ex all ending up viewing
each other's profiles on OKCupid.
The subject is the object, and the object is the subject,
though that didn't stop you from moralizing about family.
Mine laid down on the tracks,
and now tall bridges make me nervous.
Anything you want to tell me,
you can say it through a mask.
The game's rigged, anyway.
Wet roots rot in the bottom of the pot.

2)
Let's choose a route with less guns
in the window and a tug on the toga.
I'm banking on a run on the banks at the end
of a long hallway featuring doorbell chimes
of a gasmask cracking, of an even louder 4th of July,
and electroshock therapy back in fashion.
Is that what happened to my Manwich?
I'd rather have lots of whisker lickin'
and a soundtrack to the bomb squad
with flying saucers bumping into makeshift stars
because this existence is all there is
with its fluctuating ratios of signal to noise.
Then there's the one standing behind a register
selling people stuff,
or rows of rows for the butcher,
like soldiers climbing out of their foxholes
in the rain. No more future,

but I'm still glad I don't live there anymore
with its endless game of fetch.

3)
I'm not going to lie to you; actually, I might
after I deleted those old photos.
My burrito will be ready soon,
but you don't need to make it interactive;
this report card is challenging enough
with HR now automated, except for the escape key
that never works after you've pressed send,
as if this is the desert
and you've been traveling for years.
I just got here, and I'll be gone soon,
watching them steal your knife and then stab you
in the back with it.
That's enough for now.
I'll always root for the underdog.
The flight simulator is closed for the day
with its low-lying clouds graying the bracelets
loose on your wrists, slightly damaged
like the rest of us or dented.
The balm goes on your lips, curtains parted,
a temporary figure beneath the rolling pin.

4)
Here comes the sun. How many selfies do you want?
What about this one where I'm clutching
a dustpan without a handle?
We kept her Facebook page active after she died.
This is a novel about peeling skin and sticking
a banana in the tailpipe of a police van
because it's a long time until our next set
of New Year's resolutions. Mine is to wash
the dog bed, so go ahead and instruct me again—
I love it when you do that.

There's a shred in time, like a lion squatting
on your chest while you dream.
We ran circles around the island,
stopping to empty every trashcan filled
with tomorrow's excuses and braces
extracted with taffy, just as life is one big cling.
A small flag flaps from an antennae
pulling in any signal other than static and silence
with their clotting inside
missing wildly.

THE DEPRESSED THERAPIST

There's a light at the end of the chimney we use
as a periscope in reverse, sprinkling stars
like breadcrumbs in a forest beneath a leaky
ceiling. Every landscape has its own sunset.
Please tell me more, starting with knitting.
Sometimes the false logic seems better
than the real one. Anything to help settle
the crash-test dummy's stomach. The rest
is managed by computers and whatever
comments you leave on my Instagram feed.

I like watching the fireboat chug into action.
There's a violence to the hummingbird,
body hollow like a bulb skating round
and round the rink. For a while, we had to live
off of our savings, naming the ribcage Casper
or thief. Then we went three and out,
wearing a big hat and boots, because it gets
cold on the train. Where words fail, music
fills the spaces. So when are you coming over?

I'm a terror with the DMs. My heart
is expensive.

We drink vodka on the holidays to celebrate
our new ferns, our founding fathers, in a hail
of bullets and Christmas tree ornaments.
I even wore a fake beard and flannel shirt,
smelling like evergreen technology or a funny
playground. Minutes later, we stopped
on the side of the road to look under the hood,
wondering, Who brought a Super Soaker
to a sack race? We're just beads on a chain.

The free write didn't turn out to be so free,
though it's pure internet gold. What was I
thinking? I do standup at the laundromat
and current romance. My stage name
might be Haphazard or Left Shark before
the data gets collected, then Skype me in
along with chicken tenders since I got
my start in dinner theater. You might even
call it drama. Right next to the nail
is the hammer's indentation, and probably
many, or tomorrow's outrage replaces today's,
cigarette smoke curling above the guards.

I see your point, and I don't know the answer.
My scarf is a bit tight around the neck,
but almost everything softens in the tub
except this spreadsheet they gave me at work
for keeping track of celebrities wearing
baggy sweatpants and ogled beach bods.
I quickly switched to a backup plan
that involves laser tag and a mirror, although
it's what's on the inside that truly matters
according to the earnest student I once was.

I also used to be more moralistic. Now I steal
the traffic cones when no one's looking,
except for the health insurance brokers
or the drone and satellite views. Where should
I go after school? We sent the prize through
the laundry, rubbing the surfaces until
they shine like rows of fluorescent bulbs
at the office, and trying not to do more harm
than good. The signals travel farther at night,
scraping the day away and handing out cherries.
But you'll still need to call the plumber here,
power lines snapping beneath heavy snow.

THE HEART IS HEAVY LIFTING

We wake to rain,
      to the boss already at the office.
I was born for customer service,
  but I know orphans
will always want more,
       even if it's easier to edit as you go,
until whatever fruit remains
  is low hanging.
I don't have enough TV
       except where the snowman sits
leaving contrails on the couch
  like a dog's jingling collar.
The next day I found the rest
      in my slippers.

The cannibals didn't start it,
      but they'll be there at the end
while we argue over
  which pattern of curtain to hang.

I say the sky could be wider,
                              imagining a fantasy team
consisting solely of the injured
        because the earth
is really a spaceship,
                            strumming the theme to *Star Wars*
on an acoustic guitar
        until the neighbors complain,
phasers set to stun
                      and broken memories.

Now it's just called the economy
        or a steel cage where
two people get paid to beat each other up,
        and we cheer.
You can only fool the system for so long,
                                    except for
bird song and taking out the trash.
        Why did I click on that?
No wonder your favorite outfit
                                  is sweatpants surrounded
by all these rules.
        Some prizes should be given
for not even
        showing up.

BEGGING TO DIFFER

    We clean up nicely
for the parents
    but still track in history
on the bottom
    of our shoes.

It's always an anniversary
of something
    gone missing,
including the future.

That line gets me
to the next one,
    a stutter step
accompanied on bass.

The splinter stays stuck
as we sniff the narcotics
    a Waffle House away
where they seat us
    near the bathroom.

We left after
running out of butter
    because it should give
a little pleasure
    before the police
summon Strongman & White.

There's a flicker
in the power supply
    putting the grid
on high alert.

Eventually the arms give out
while treading water,
    wetting the flares
in our pocket.

Kids in bars,
my own included,
    counting down from

a thousand spilled beers
    to anywhere except here.

    I got a job fluffing
pillows for the rich
    and giving out bro hugs.

    When I sleep,
I'll sleep for a long time,
    or you can appease me
with candy and a hammer.

    Billboards flap past,
delivering us to the system
    and its plug-and-play casinos.

    It's the big lie
of the American dream.
    You're only telling it
more calmly.

CONSTITUTIONAL CRISIS

My ode to joy has a sinus infection.
We stole a roll of toilet paper
because it's come to that,
though we only used it to wipe off the screen.
In this way, everything is connected.
The difference between the two is the text you send,
not the one I just sent my ex.
Next up: doing the dishes.
I take booster shots to the jaw
before going on vacation at the spelling bee
where I forgot the "i" in professional.

Metallic clock hearts beat to Benzedrine,
but some days you never quite wake up,
which isn't the same as not wanting
to be hungover again.

There's an ON/OFF switch, and then there's the plug.
Frogs have so much pucker.
Everybody's going, but no one was there,
so which distress signal should we answer?
I pick the one that comes from the beach.
Certain bridges you can walk to;
this one is here in my room,
and home is somewhere in between.
Language got gum on it.
There are crime scenes that never get solved
as a river slowly carves away at an island
where only stalks are left from a harvest
hauled away in trucks, including song,
with just enough left over for us to snack on
or else use for kindling.

How many words does it take to say we're lost?
Or that the roofers arrived a day too late?
You pulled your autumn sweater out of the dryer
to signal a change in seasons.
I tied more knots in the rope.
Yet it's a busy period for deliveries,
and I'm not talking about the holidays.
I put all my ducks in a row, and they each say quack.
I hate getting yelled at by the dentist,
even though every poem is a ghost,
not the gold sticker I received for a grave—
I mean, grade—as night hardens around it.
We got along, and then we didn't.
It started when your dog ate my flu shot,
and spiraled downward from there.

I know it's a challenge to date someone with kids,
but at least you're never alone.
There's also an app for that.
At some point you have to leave the ranch
if you want to catch stars with your mouth,
and I wouldn't say all the good jobs are taken,
yet people are sleeping in their cars.
I've done that while driving cross-country,
waking up to fireworks and rain.
The last time I checked, hugs were free,
though let's be honest,
everything about that guy is kinda dickish.
And you thought junior high school was bad.
I can't see my face and its little factories.
A police shooting is redundant.

When did we let the landlords and bankers take over?
My head hurts from the screaming inside,
as the weather went from bad to worse.
So, too, did the candidates.
I tried to keep up, but you're holding the money;
mine got tied up in a tax on swampland.
I donated my car to help the homeless
but ended up with a dented fender
after you pulled up to the bumper,
as we stay awake with the machines.
My nickname is Berry Crumble,
but pumping the brakes only makes it worse,
as the damage took years to repair,
while eliminating the mid-range
and the helmet's reflective tape and logo.

On one desk is an ocean; on the other, a set of keys.
Something in the air coats my tongue.
The last time I visited, it was warm,
so don't wrap the hat so tightly.

Doom—because I like the word.
The swollen conquerors topple in their girth.
There's no channel to change when it's all one feed,
as my deep dish got traded for a tuber,
keeping me light on my feet
after the gardeners gave electroshock therapy
to the rototiller and poppies.
Squirrels bury nuts in the lawn,
because you can't keep it on a leash.
Or maybe it's time to wash the sock puppet—
mine has a floppy tongue; yours, an eye to the side.

I watch the light fade without a metaphor.
My hands go numb with crayon.
Who let the sharks loose in the swimming pool?
We deplete our survival kit of Halloween candy
and Band-Aids, of broken doorbells,
so give a shout from the street when you're ready to go.
Let's make the office pretend.
I read evil backwards, but trouble finds us,
just as the comedy was unintentional,
although I can see why you might laugh
now that the most me wins.
I'd rather take a backhoe to the yard, then the stage.
Oranges stack in a neat pyramid
until the next monkey ambles along,
the one sharing our haircut and DNA.

Yet I hold onto green like that tree across the street.
I'm holding onto the noise.
My credit score went up when I ate too many donuts.
Before Iowa there was only hardship,
but we're each a drone strike away,
though some much more than others.
No wonder I'm all about that bass beneath the window,
because nothing is transparent.

Boys don't wash the stain from my heart.
Besides, you remind me of beer.
The refrigerator doesn't hum, it rattles,
along with everything on top and inside,
and maybe you and me too,
our spines adrift against a flickering screen
featuring sports and reports from the wars.

PICK OF THE LITTER

To the ends of the earth we go
without ever leaving the mall.
Later, I got taken to the cleaners.
The moon wanders in stages,
just as there are times I miss you
so much it hurts, as we forget
about the wars until we're reminded.
Or like a giraffe given a yank
on the leash, we're all neck,
riding the freight elevator to work.

How else am I supposed to transport
this dip? Screw the charm factor
and grab the power from those who
don't use it for good. We hear
the sirens before we see them,
casting a rope ladder into the wind.
That's not the same as a sugar
hangover, but I refuse to kiss the ring
and try to keep my grave clean—
otherwise called the curbside follies.

That wasn't very funny either,
and this truck is blocking my view

as well as a fire escape framing
the poverty rainbow. Not poverty,
I mean positivity. One love.
Yet I don't know the arrival time,
and the sun is setting where the sea
meets the desert at a virtual horizon.
How does a cartoon character die?
Frame by frame.

WORSE THAN NORMAL

I used Groupon to pay for a cruise,
    then paddled behind in a dinghy.
We get to dine at the captain's table
    whenever he's away.
That's when you showed me
    how to walk a lobster
before breaking down in tears,
    as I count the rows
to the emergency exit because
    there's only one wing on this plane.

We drove to the center of the city,
    but it doesn't exist.
Yet rejection still stings, making words
    out of letters found
in the dumpster behind Fish and Fancy,
    stirring the cinders like a soup.
There are cupcakes for celebrating
    that day too, and punch by the ladle
tapped against your chest in place of
    an expectorant or wood rot or I'm sorry.

Next up, the song of the summer,
    and this email I really shouldn't send,
the way an octopus gives a hug
    to the hurt machine.
It might be easier to draw a picture,
    although it's important to accessorize
with glue guns and plastic,
    with health clinic waiting lines,
with imitation star charts,
    and sleeping pills next to the bed.

GOING OVER THE WALL

The echo in the door says goodbye
like pelts in a row at the trading post.
I finished all the treats in the basket,
though now we're having trouble digging out.

Next up is the blizzard dance
and whatever's at hand for smashing.
This includes the Pied Piper
when the rats will follow almost anyone.

But I'm heading into the wind;
in the other direction, you don't even need a hat.
This might be the first storm of the year,
yet there will be plenty more to come.

So go ahead and stock up on pretzels and beer.
I'll take lemonade and a bruise.
Or maybe it's the days of wine and roses
deciphered in the shadows cast by a match.

That's the psychology of the divining rod,
hands reaching for a tremor
written right into the slippage
and open late until they shut us down.

THE FOUNDLINGS

We moved offshore to escape the flooding except
the only thing to drink is salty while engines melt
the clouds. You can't handle the truth says the guy
in uniform, but I haven't believed in it since you left,
and you could have gone sooner. There's a finite
amount of highway, though it's still pretty huge.
All those daisies won't cover up the stench
or survive the reopening of the Locust Club.
It's like a cloak for our sadness I threw into a field
along with a sign that reads BACK IN 5 MINUTES,
even if not really. By the way, who's the hippie
with the lighter fluid? I ate Facebook and out came
Twitter, from which I got tossed like Earl Weaver
arguing a call in spring training, because sometimes
that feels right too, art upsetting the do-gooders.

Let's say that I've been naïve about some things
and not about others, but acid reflux is a constant.
I must like the look of this rubble, and these teams
aren't even trying to win. I know, funny, right?
I thought it might be political; you said personal,
as the lights turn on in the middle of the day,
which isn't the same as years passing between
Google Alerts and the super glue I used to fix
a tooth or my wireless keyboard after banging it
against the ceiling. Why is that television character
talking to me? This is so embarrassing. But I'm not

waiting to be saved by a plate of cookies nicknamed
Dinky Doodle or String to the Dinghy. Instead,
pink clouds slowly roll in, droopy-lidding the sky
until we can't go home again.

It's warmer outside than it is in here, but I can't see
anything past the feed lot with its antennas rusting
in the yard replaced by a more efficient stream
linking the pulleys. The video chat brings us closer,
or at least shows me inside your room. We disabled
the other features, like keeping the daffodils from
toppling on their stems, yellow flares in slow motion
eventually breaking through the soil. We do too,
as the wind gets tangled in the branches, helicopters
hovering above where margarine is an entry-level oil.
My Sephora tote bag. My box of Special K.
The commute takes over an hour, while we count
lollipops strewn on the floor, sticky to everything except
our mouths as language lodges with the chewy.

Don't forget to breathe, and if you're lucky you'll lose
track of time until the next commercial interrupts
the roaming kiss cam with its alumni network of one
junior college transfer. The rest go into business
while we stay amateurs until the end, and all that
separates us is our epidermis. The early bird might
get the worm, but what about the nightcrawlers?
You preferred brunch to inchoate and blue where
the next scene is called a redo. Then what happened?
More of the same—not an imaginary war
but a war on the imagination, and everything
less free, including the dream shake knocking over
the uprights. You can have the rest, though don't
neglect to put a stamp on the letter a little faster.
We range far in a day and speak in different tongues.

SOFT TARGETS

All the messages have to be approved first,
        but occasionally one slips through;
this time it's a sideline rant before
        the sedation squad arrives only to fall
        on their own swords.
Fur-clad French trappers ate beaver while humming
        under a plastic tarp during the whole ride home
        after a flood destroyed the boiler.
At least that's the view from the Hindenburg
        as it slowly plummets to earth.

I keep one ventricle illuminated in blue—
        the others in green and white.
Nobody in the bar knows;
in fact, I'm not even sure it's true.
The distractions are so numerous,
        you can't even call them that,
while the future is fantastical and wrapped in tissue paper
        that shreds when wet or smeared with lotion,
then gets put on a pile of trash literally reaching
        to the moon.

Small moths wait for me to put the sweaters away
        before sitting down to dinner.
My Skype app doesn't seem to be working.
We went to the theater without leaving the house,
        every little I firing its musket ball
        as part of the reenactment.
No wonder I can't write a short story.
There's sand in my shoes, but as long as
        it's not between my teeth, answering that
        Charles Atlas comic book ad was totally worth it.
Now I split the seams while you simply split.

Plus, there's all that hurt to carry around.
Or else we're blotted, and I'm poking at my ribs
        before the crows do, mind in a different place
        while warming up the seat cushion
        or inflating the life vest.
Which flight are you on, anyway?
The monogrammed binoculars are out of focus,
        like first thought best thought
        except when it's not.

That's one way to chip the polish.
Soon there will be nothing left to steal.
The number 14 has always been good to me
        excluding that competitive eating contest.
Oh, pinch me, I must be dreaming.
We might move the words around,
yet the logic remains the same, such as changing
        the names of Santa's reindeer before
        they go off script and the drones lock and load
        from a cubicle in Florida.

OPEN SEASON

The big ready heads this way,
but it's more like a Ferris wheel
spinning atop a chop shop
with a pastry business on the side
opening the passenger door
into traffic as the cat drags in
whatever it dug up in the yard,
since now it costs money to see
the sun or sip the water, so I'm
grateful for anything that comes
in a slim pack or puts the nose
to the nose while waiting for

the hunting apparel catalog to arrive,
because these days it can only
be a bonus to look good in orange
for the riverkeepers' holiday party
quietly pushing the boat from
the bank as ripples part from the prow
and drainage pipes lining the route
with their runoff used for chicken feed
and disposable horses—I mean,
general dystopia—but don't tell that
to the fire brigade pushing ladders
against the clouds while debating
fair use and the restoration of public
space at a mall wiping away
the snowflakes, just as last year it was
Abercrombie & Fitch, this year
it's Hollister, next year a solstice shadow
slithering down the temple steps
or drinking lots of beer, I don't
really know, and my lungs are almost
broken from these letters, most of them
unsent or read by the neighbors,
but that's okay, because everyone's
a neighbor with or without secrets
while the heat captured in the pollen
puts the bees in a frenzy during
their search and then the journey home
with its unusual shake 'n bake,
its confusing crisper drawer slid beneath
a FOR SALE sign swinging on loose
hinges, and that's no metaphor
in this era of foreclosures, or maybe
it's both, leaving submerged wrecks
to form coral reefs or crashing a car
into a garden to make a seedbed
for the next set of renovations.

UNTITLED

We're on the verge of extinction.

EVICTION NOTICE

The clanging buoy sunk out of earshot where
the recent amputee tingles a phantom limb,
although I forget the name of the movie
in which the hero gets clubbed with a prosthetic.
The soundtrack for that is when you mention
your debt, or maybe it's a trumpet and cheese grater
substituting for the army and its orderly mess hall
because no amount of discipline will compose
these spaces cloudy with alcohol and a juice cleanse
while the cat litter gets on everything, yet the scarcity
still haunts us.

The week after that we'll be visiting our parents
and their left to the imagination, left to whatever
we can spell in sand on the beach of this flyover
while waving at the hometown booster
hoisting the flag to half-mast and other stuff lost
where we fall: cold medicine, earrings,
the Death Star trench, regular haircuts, and loofahs.
Then it's on to the next one and incisions
stolen from time off the clock. I go numb
just thinking about it, and only get up early
when I have to, even if I keep the curtains pulled open
like a spill on the floor.

The secret is that there's no secret. Life is brutal
and short. Plug it up with a nosegay as mammals hunt
each other's fear locking the door to a mudslide

behind them and ignoring the fine print.
That's on one channel; another is just for kids
or shows cars racing around an asphalt oval spanning
our names on a list. Next to them is a drawing
of an appetite. Seeds planted now ripen later,
while the tractor is all claws a few inches above
the aquifer and trailed by a flock of magpies that winter
behind the zoo and Joe Namath's fur coat.

I'm waiting for the kerosene delivery, which is the plot
for another *Home Alone* sequel, for rainy Sundays.
Yours is for a poorly concealed rage I'll give one coat
of paint to like gymnasts do, taping off the corners
or propped up with crutches, rubber tips worn
from lumbering up and down the stairwell,
then accidentally run over by the fire chief driving
a late model Suburban with tinted windows.
I'm putting my hands up at the concert, but now
what should I do? I don't know any of the words
to this song.

BETWEEN TWO POINTS

1)
I have come to the end of this,
the end of ruffling winter,
     the end of designations
killing sheep to appease the winds
and every stupid thing
     done to daughters.

     I'd give them the world if I could.

2)
Where's the game being played?
Somewhere that closes after dark.
Each poem is ghostwritten
as a thousand trees without mercy,
    a series of stopgap repairs.

    I feel it in the face.
    I feel it in the hustle.

3)
You try to stay away from your addictions,
yet find yourself next to a lake
    that the words stopped speaking.
They also keep the rain off
    as the comb is to Disney.

I've been away too long.

I will meet you there.

4)
I dropped my cake behind the bed.
Please don't steal my shoes.

Love is the one constant.

I'm a long edge against
a blunting surface
while the curve of us extends
    past the orbits.

5)
Boyhood is a ridiculous suitcase.
The red amaryllis needs more light.
All hurt is ordinary.

We watched the whole movie
    in four-minute clips,
then played the piano
    with forearms and fists.

6)
The stars align, although
    I can't see them.
Airline pilots also practice at home.
The helmets go missing
    with meaning.
The music is ugly, but I don't mind.

No more is my head a stew.

7)
The shoreline isn't getting any closer.

I could stare at this screen for hours,
watching smokestacks pierce the clouds.

Only the tombstone and microphone float
when the delivery system
    is working. Open vein.
A banner for the rally.

A SERIES OF SMALL FAVORS

Someone hid the panic button,
                          so instead we dance
    with the other skeletons,
eye sockets sloshing with drank-the-Kool-Aid
    and getting grease stains
                          on the shiny counters.
You called it watersports and reached for your surfboard;
    I scrambled to find the saltines.
The new neighbors are already moving out,
    and if the bridge collapses,
                          I will too,
because I'm tired of living on this houseboat
    even if the waters are rising,
and I finally made a down payment
                          on a condo in Georgia
where I'll sing a song of myself in a swamp,
    and I'll sing it on Dexedrine.
                          Just try to stop me.
Holy shit, this poem needs a revision.
Like a Tumblr rapper, I played it for easy rhymes
    and cheap laughs,
                          though that's a better use of technology
    than the day traders.
The western black rhino is now officially extinct (Nov. 2013),
    along with a bug I've never heard of,
but there are still moments
                          when I long to be replaced
    by a more difficult movement.
Or else there's no grain in the wood
                              because the wood isn't real,
yet don't let that stop you from using it for kindling
    now that the thermometer is dropping.
Where was I?
Oh, yeah, battling the salt lick.

You wiped a burger on it,
                        as the grass bends gently in the breeze
   after swallowing a muscle relaxant.
That's ridiculous,
             except you should have seen
   what I tried to hack into a glider.
We improvise the tools from whatever
                          hasn't been sold or stolen.
We look forward to seeing our friends.
Please make sure you say good-bye
                      before you leave,
   and put a can of food out for the cat.
It's the art of the hustle
             that gets you farther,
the collection of plastic zippers,
                    and a noonday sun spiking the sky.
Better than my orange juice at breakfast,
                        I guess.
Claw marks indicate the escape route
   while the flicker keeps us in place.
That's how we get traction in the sand,
                          inhaling clouds of exhaust.

POSTCARDS FROM PARADISE

We make the undertow easy to reach,
then fill it with stars,
or as the drunk astronomer calls them—
dumpsters for the soul.
No wonder pronouns are confusing
when all of it made me.
Now I practice the art of loss
until I get it right.

I stepped on a metronome
after slipping on cooking oil and Philip Morris.
My head went missing,
and it's yours to find,
but you have to break the internet first.
Isn't that necklace called a choker?
I'm tired of this dirty corner.
History is its own stain.

Besides that, I can't find my keys.
I'd store them under my hat
if it warmed more than phlegm
and everything viscous and glistening
when the carcass is slit open.
I'm your weekend warrior with a knee brace
cheering on the last to finish.
I like being back here amid the branches.

SHELTER FROM THE STORM (FOUND POEM)

Excellent clean room.
Right across from a wonderful diner.
Mcdonalds right next door.
On the other side is a drug store and a laundromat.
WHat more could you want?

PRODUCT PLACEMENT

The heart on my sleeve is a calf's
because *Vogue* tells me it's the latest fashion,
not the white Keds and jeans popular again
this year. I rode the shuttle in circles

to the airport, mixing some horizontal into
the vertical weave, or else we're ground down
by time despite packing the whole cold forest
in a cooler and reprising Evel Knievel jumping stuff
at the breeder's intersection of kitsch and cliché,
at the Bonneville Salt Flats and Miracle-Gro.

After that, she sold the mopeds for drug money,
and who could blame her, really?
The next book we read will have lots of pictures,
or maybe it's just called a movie.
The phantom is a way of saying no,
tugging on your ear the way parents do
to a troublesome kid. Otherwise,
we pretend to be self-made. We wait
for the small green buds to emerge,
the new tulips trimmed to fit in jars and vases.

You still smelled like smoke two days
after sitting near the fire in black boots
laced up high in the heat
like the arsonist hidden in each of us.
I'm sorry I ate the last piece of chocolate
while not matching my shoes and belt
and invoking the tuck rule,
but I've had it up to here if I stack
all the stools in this enormous bar,
and if that's the best you got, then of course
you'll want to check with the officials.

300 billion served and counting pretty much
brings us up to date, adding padding
to the hamster wheel about to get bumpy
for the one we named Squeaky Fromme
or else it's wads of polyester clouding the air
after a pillow fight with the nurse practitioners

that started with a gentle reflex-test tap tap tap
to the knee. They said the hip replacement
should arrive in the mail soon, so you can show me
where to insert it along with a hamburger wrapper
found at baggage claim.

The words are waiting for me, even when
I'm away, just as it gets noisy on this block,
especially in the summer. Yet I'm not here
to impress you with my book collection;
in fact, you can have that too along with
a fresh coat of paint and doubling over.
Closing time is another form of moving,
and for the rich I'll be the chip sniffer.
Let the light shine through one day,
not the fox composing a portrait of the hen house.
Admit it, sometimes you just want to flee.

No wonder, given the new voting restrictions
and your patent permanently pending.
Weather patterns look smaller on the map,
and I can see our old house from space.
We take on vertigo with the fringe dangling
from your purse, with a set of pills and the letters
carved into them like some kind of soup,
whether sans serif, suddenly salad,
or sponge baths in a hammock.
I don't really have an answer for that.

Seven people were shot in South Chicago this weekend.
The event planner exists only on Facebook.
It's a little early in the day for Mister Softee
to be idling at the corner, but sugar needs a ride,
so don't sleep on it at the warning track dirt
with Donald Duck slobber.
Instead, let the female bassist sing.

I see the needle quiver as it pierces the skin
and the curtain covering our dreams knitted
by havoc—that thrum on our throat simultaneously
slipping the sunglasses to the top of our head.

The foreclosures resulted in a mountain of drywall.
At Kroger, they call me The Glue.
You spelled it confession while taking the legs out.
There's nothing distinguished about that rifle,
and it left a stain on the rug.
The police are eager to get through when
it's not migrating birds swerving around
the nuclear reactor cracking in CGI
with drinks on the patio, flouting a spoiler alert
for the latest branding iron forged in an ice age.
It's always war that makes history real.

CAVITY CREEP

1)
The pen may be mightier
than the sword, but not *that* sword.
I was a conscientious objector
during the battle of the bands
where I checked in on Foursquare
to upload my data.
My little collective shares
a bag of rice and the dialectic
of utopia and critique.
I forget what time class lets out
until I hear the children's voices,
with free rides in a submarine
pulled along the canal
by a donkey coaxed with a fritter

after drought in the heartland
decimated the carrot crop.
We live in a culture of substitutions,
including me and you.
Everything spilling and planned
obsolescence. Or blood for the guns.

2)
We cover the runway with paper
to mark each landing,
then return to our day job
and find our apartment emptied
when we get home,
the dog's breath warm in the cold.
I treasured each moment of it,
though I'm not the one
with the migraines,
and some cavities aren't the result
of too much sweetness
but instead from drilling down.
I saw this on the Lifetime channel
and its history of toppled needs
framed by billowing smokestacks
and featuring everyone
the movie *Kids* made famous.
Don't take delight
in another's misfortunes.
Don't aim the server at my head.

3)
We're one click away
from being celebrities,
and that includes your pet.
Is honey more expensive now
because all the bees are dying?
I'm trying to figure out

cap and trade with an online
calculator generating random numbers
like old ads for prostitutes in London
phone booths, hands shaky
after drinking five Red Bulls.
Yet whatever we win
at the carnival costs them
less to produce it.
That doesn't include expenses
for the father's funeral or
black cars we drive through the night.
Time always eats first,
even when you race it to the table
in overalls with their built-in bib.
On Sundays I wear them
with a matching hat.

4)
Golf's on. This room is filling up
with ghosts, and I haven't
gotten to the cafeteria.
That's different from arguing
with no one in particular
while cleaning up the cookie dough,
each word in place of an emotion
that inappropriately kisses on the lips.
Still, karma is a logic,
not a revenge mechanism.
Butterflies land where you pour
orange juice on your skin,
at least the ones flitting in a net
and hopped up on vaporized DayQuil.
Gossip flies as fast
as you can text it.
Tell them we'll be repairing holes
in the wall at 3 a.m., sandwiched

by a drink and the light
I've learned to live for.
I don't care when you arrive,
just as long as you make it.

DAMAGE IS DONE

TREES FOR THE FOREST

My only piece of advice is, Get more honey.
Otherwise, it's long days at the dude ranch
with lots of grilling, though I wouldn't
trust him behind the wheel. Stop, dog, stop,
my daughter used to say while I was driving
in slippers, not those Prada loafers we bought
your dad for his birthday with a grid coordinating
the wreck and fingers colder at the tips.

We were lucky to escape that one with minor
damage, even if the entire apartment now needs
a new paint job or wallpaper imprinted
with your favorite team's logo, as long as
it's not the Outhouses or the Rorschachs.
I've got better ways to spend my time,
like removing crust from the bread and dialing
a toll-free number for a spittoon near the ivy.

Please don't take me to your leader, because
I've already ridden on a spaceship,
and maybe once was drunk on a bicycle
when I was younger after too much
Crème de menthe, except I wouldn't quote me.

For now, I'll let you have all the words,
not including fluff, which I'm keeping
after you gave the parrot a spin on the Roomba.

Instead, I could try to paint a picture. First,
I'll need a toothbrush and a dustpan. No rainbows,
though it might be for the best. There are paths
that are more of a wander, and bones used for clubs.
If you look closely, you can see the follicles,
the hunger setting in with the meal and a waver
in the day that used to arrive in a tumble
like Paul Bunyan striking a giant matchstick.

OPEN ALL NIGHT

My fresh start entails getting taken to the cleaners
because who leaves the dark on during the day?
Everything is almost like camping.
Yet I try to give death a wide berth
since it's coming soon enough
though we still ended up lingering
in the crosswalk as mouth breathers.
To the desert, I'm known as Sporty Spice,
but Sparkles is a male model's name.
I went back to school for unlearning,
which is harder than it seems.

The clouds aren't moving in the right direction,
or maybe it's just me.
The salt lining follows us far from the sea,
like throwing flowers at a doorstep
until the cops yank their guns from the holster.
Turns out the body is made of glass

ripping through the bottom of a bag.
I've seen it once or twice
when the house gets taken away.
You can watch by clicking on a link.

THE COURTESY INTERVIEW

There isn't a cheap room left to rent
                                      in this city,
    but those strollers sure take up a lot of space.
The bartender calls me Toots,
                                  except I don't play the horn;
        I play the mine as a redaction.
We used to talk all night on the phone,
    returning the spaghetti to sender.
Just don't hit me with those rolled-up blueprints.
Better to keep power visible,
                                  loading bombs under the wing.
I need a garden hose and water.
The music box is way out of tune.

We forgot the landscape is lunar
                                  at the roadside colonial,
    fields of corn burned to a stubble.
At some point,
        we'll have to finish the laundry
    and pay to have our teeth scraped.
You can do it gently or I can gag on it;
either way,
        I'm going to have to rinse,
            then assemble a house out of plastic,
    that is, everything excluding the roof.
Some captains only see the dry dock.

The coroner has a different version,
                              one the animals hold,
          fingers curling to the palm.

The train left before we got there.
It's quiet beneath the snow.
What we love gets lodged
                    in the heart,
but I don't know why
                  since it's so dark in there.
      Or maybe because it's leaky,
              like an emergency room intake.
You could ask the junkie squatters on my block.
The law always arrives in force,
          collecting bracelets for the ride.
Every day is award season
                      for the kite on a two-foot string.

Yet we're still faster than a download,
                              sipping Mountain Dew.
You've got me all up in my feelings.
The eraser is there for the taking,
                as certain memories make my head hurt,
        giving the pith helmet a good spin.
Let me finish my Froot Loops first
                        before the milk makes them soggy,
      a path wet beneath the snail.
It's the process, not the product,
                          where true freedom lies,
        piling our luggage by the door.

LAKE OF DREAMS

        I have a costume for each occasion, a snow day
for every school. It's difficult to criticize the ocean, but I'll take
parasailing at twenty feet. There's a wolf prowling outside the walls.
Who needs a watch anymore? My smartphone beeps on the second,
so now I never lose track of time or when the next payment is due,
since nothing here comes for free, including these comment streams,
where we count off at morning
                                          roll call. I stuff a bayonet into
a sack full of hay and hide behind a plate of noodles, as the fury
of a nation makes the wheat fields wave. We need noise to fall asleep,
though I don't mean sneezing. It's morning on one side of the globe,
while closer to home I vote for rent is too damn high and a rant.
The heat tests us and the poplar, our faces pressed in close against
the storefront glass.

        I'd stop for a moment and make us a sandwich, but you
sent the lunchmeat to the cleaners, declaring the end can't come
soon enough before unfastening your seatbelt while crossing
the bridge, because that's the closest we'll get to flying until
someone invokes the mercy rule. With the money we inherited,
we could build a sandbox with a scratchpad. Meanwhile,
I think I'll sleep in the car
                                          or maybe start to work on my tan.
That's the crushing thing—the rest fades away or gets replaced,
yet the Ritalin makes me jittery, cutting the stem too close
to the bloom, to the cement mixer. In other words, keep on trucking,
as long as there's a cup holder for the syrup and a chance to gun
the motor while stuck in neutral. If not, we'll improvise with faulty
knowledge, with a picture of a picture on Snapchat.

        The armies are in revolt, and that's not very twee,
leaning a sound cannon into the ear. We decorate the school gym
with aquariums for the dance, as this year's theme is going under;
then it got canceled by a drought. In any case, joy is proportional

to disappointment, like holding senior prom in the early afternoon.
Some dogs say woof and some say arf. The smell can be a bit
overwhelming, from Narnia
                                to the trash can. I found myself stating,
Nice suit, as loud thunder rattles the windows and a swing set
rolls away with the tumbleweeds, zombies of whatever marching
across the plains, giving dopamine a reuptake or flush with authority.
Who owns the house we live in? I used to imagine another world;
now I eat the log cabin in a video game featuring the last family farm
in Nebraska.

     I'm a temporary trend, a hum giving away our position,
just as your pink hat isn't keeping the bees at bay, and lock and load
is never seamless. Yet somewhere there's a shiny spaceship waiting
for each of us, an expressway to the skull rapped on by the father's
knuckles at the door before the law while I get the teleprompter greasy,
ruining the big speech and preferring to toast the pudding.
My friend calls them DILFs
                                at Lowe's or Home Depot.
The next day, the sun came out and deliveries resumed, although
I still don't know your name. I trip over the iambs; I'm the prosody
accompanying a vacuum cleaner around the kitty litter and stuff
like that, so please teach me control. You can bring your spouse,
but don't forget a bag for the planets, as the doctor's police call box
interdimensionally spins.

     Right about now we could use a better backup plan after
dropping our contact lenses on the rug and raking loose change
in the yard, otherwise designated a spill zone despite repeated trips
to the Container Store for more plastic bins. They don't compost,
but I do. Weezy makes me think of *The Jeffersons* and Lil Wayne.
Mom paid for lunch while I smoked outside in khakis, hoping
that in an emergency we can shatter
                                the rear window with a golf club.
We teach the history of decay as the wedding photographer herds
everyone onto the cliff where I hid the Fig Newtons and gasmasks

within an entire bioregion under threat, your hair pulled back tight
in a bun. I've walked for hours, though I'm not much of a hiker,
fresh cobwebs draped across the trail every morning like stories
or your torn Led Zeppelin t-shirt.

       The invaders can be plants or nations draining a duck pond
built with a backhoe and laryngitis, with workers during a shift change
when McDonald's introduces spa services featuring cold masks
with rubdowns and automated slaughter. There are overalls for adults,
rounded clasps sliding gently over the metal buttons. Sports highlights
are next before wiping the seat with fat drippings while the warden
is distracted by jellyfish blooms
                                     in warming oceans. Or maybe
it was your frankfurter that dropped on the bathmat as a drone
tracked it. The ring of trash around the earth also circles my head,
although one day it will dissolve into strings of light, like you
and like me. The pigeons return to where they hatched years ago,
but now there are snakes on a plane landing at an airport deemed
international because it's close to Canada, as natural as cologne.

       I'd sprint from here to the finish line, except I don't see it—
those giraffes ducking hovering helicopters are blocking my view
during a summer of cursing. Next summer promises to be even worse.
For thousands of years soldiers have attacked the gates of Baghdad,
as history shrinks to the present moment, except for the slippery moss
we step on at the bottom of the lake, the frogs summoning us back
to shore with cries both throaty
                                  and shrill, or else it's mating season.
The stacked plywood eventually fused into a solid cube, then a UFO
flew through it. TV pundits rarely face repercussions, but at least
the Holiday Inn where we're staying has a bar with Hubble telescope
motif pointing toward the bibs. I don't remember anything after that
while waiting for the officers to arrive in a round of friendly fire
scattering my seashell collection and streaks of Lemon Pledge.

The best way to cross the river is not to tarry or struggle.
Turns out Robbie is a girl. I placed a begging bowl in heaven,
but it won't stop the ruckus. That's why my Twitter handle
is @digdeep since @waxonwaxoff was taken. I stayed up late
making extra potato salad for your visit. Children come forward
with so much love, running toward the thwarted, as the messengers
arrive late or are ignored, then
                           smash the banjos where the strings
tap parchment. Wasn't that a scene on *Family Guy*? Meanwhile,
I schmoozed the laundry basket, digital rights committee, dirty money,
your hip surgery, and whatever rhymes with capsize. Read my lips,
I second the opposition, though who nixed the beer run or Ricky's
favorite rosé carried in a yarn bag to the Renaissance Faire hosted
in a 7-Eleven parking lot? I'm pretty sure it wasn't me.

        I went to the beach and forgot to bring something to read.
A single green buoy clanks in the harbor like an ambulance stuck
in traffic, its siren a swizzle to the stick. You keep the ears fuzzy
and shake out pressed flowers as exterminators squirt the perimeter
with rusty canisters and a sex grenade. Back on the island, every
salad spinner synchronized, removing drizzle from the green.
If I was a type of haircut,
                          I'd be a bob, but the conditioner makes
my hair limp, tries to pat pat pat the pain away. The next cargo ship
doesn't arrive for a week, as we pile cases of Diet Coke dockside
and the seagulls build their nests. Last winter we pretended to play tennis
but mostly nude wrestled on the couch. This time wasn't much different,
except now someone else collects the data on my downloads avoiding
anything subtitled "The Squeakquel."

        The jawbone swings like a year. My dental records are a mess,
with Luther Vandross smoothing out the edges along the thread of
taking it day to day, paycheck to paycheck, as we never quite noticed
the flickering neon until after we moved in, though it keeps the candy
awake. I guess you could feel hopeful. The epidermis is a thin cape
or a wiggle, and the return of the repressed is last night's dinner

unless it comes with Vicodin
                                for falling off my horse after experiencing
separation anxiety in reverse. That won't save me from the library
and its selected ambient works, like jiggling the handle on a toilet,
but I'm briefly free in the desert of our choosing, not magical thinking,
which is closer to OCD. A deer ate the potted plants, leaving the stems
for desperate stoners, and I'll be surprised by something when I wake up,
if only the pillow soaked with tears.

    The silk ribbons are meant to disguise the jerky; so, too,
the family man kicking over the grill. Poetry is a bird acting wounded
in order to draw predators away from its young. We build shelters
with leftovers and decorate with black box recorders, with apples
and oranges. I need you, but it shows like shoes. Snow covered
the peaks throughout the summer; we saw them across ranchland
while driving west to Denver.
                                My copy of the trip isn't numbered;
I don't even know where it went, although you're more than welcome
to autograph the satellite dish right below dreamy Ryan Seacrest
while hanging a picture crooked. One day my computer will talk to me
and then this whole place will come alive like maxed-out credit cards
and not answering the phone, but when it all gets to be too much,
I chant Deepak Chopra over and over.

    Or else I think about species that have recently gone extinct.
Hello? Is this thing working? I see the dark encroaching as the sun
slides over the house, yet smell is the sense of fear. You can drop
the rest into the sink, minus the commodore and snap peas we pin
to his shoulders, which barely slowed down the authorities or cat video
links. Look, that one fell into its food bowl! No wonder the hat keeps
slipping, although the apron
                                fits snugly, like meat to the cleaver
and its wind beneath my wings. The worst days are when we go to work;
I'd rather water my rock garden on the weekends the way history did
after storing old photo albums in the garage and made me an ugly king.
It's also my alibi regarding my whereabouts while low clouds bend

the branches back, otherwise known as pneumonia or the Ivy League takes care of its own.

      That's about when you went to visit your parents for a week. The geology is older than the bones. The pilot survived, but not a girl on the beach, while, I swear, a man with a walker took six minutes to cross the street. The filtration system is barely working, and numbers crunching is for machines after Amazon rented out the museum. Just don't call me Stumpy before laying your head on the rails, because lots of kids don't get enough
                                    to eat. A few live on this block, where cop cars escort a parade and we wave little sparklers, even in the daylight. I'll buy whatever cereal is on sale, and spend a long time standing in line. The trail leads to a pond full of turtles in the mud's sleep chamber dreaming of hydroplanes and Metamucil. The obvious rhyme would be me too, except I don't have a signature move, besides maybe getting taken down in the backfield.

      We'll find the cash however we can, and spend most of it on Skittles, while grumbling something about dudes, as the shelling of civilians continued. Baseball's trade deadline is fast approaching, though it's all so obscure, the lightning flashing behind smokestacks and the corridors empty except for a couple broken wheelchairs next to an industrial mop. Thank you for keeping it safe with conflicting messages, with my willow collection from
                                  central casting, my not-a-morning person, my closet full of one-piece jumpsuits, my thumb smudge on the horizon, my renovated dog sled. I like to relax in a cold bath, but the bubbles get distracting, especially after a gun discharged, and now everything is feeling leaky. I'm the housekeeper, shoving a rag through PayPal. The space ghost knows, leaving the rest of us to empty buckets until the check arrives. I'll need your help to get there.

      We're gigantic to our hearts, but keep the windows shut to quiet the engines. I own at least six distinct varieties of heirloom tomato, some knitted with lace, others carved from stone after I accidentally

crashed a dump truck into Mount Rushmore. That's almost a true story featuring a lid for the garbage, except I couldn't tell it any other way. In an alternative version, I drove off a cliff or else I'm kneeling roadside while fixing a flat in the rain,
                              as drugs do the waterproofing. Nevertheless, it's a world full of farthers. It's a slow creep. It is without doubt a loosened lug nut. It's also vast, open spaces where we trade the horse for the saddle. You installed a trellis for decoration, threading plastic roses through the gaps and our harvest of Styrofoam that a dolphin balances on its flipper to a steady drumbeat, though not the one honoring Our Lady of the Snows. Critter camp was mostly bugs and such.

    I can't give the book away until I check a quote. I washed a monster truck with a napkin. Everyone on our school bus teased the girl who did farm chores, mud splattered on the hem of her dress, though we're made of stars, even if I don't always know where the pain comes from. There's no narrative in that, only a fractured world amid the mergers and acquisitions and inequality built into the system, tugging the go-kart engine cord
                              before the wedding reception runs out of icing and we get our hearing checked at the clinic. That's rude justice for you, or a tremor before the quake, but maybe you can convince your parents to cosign on the lease. I've got my money tied up in funding a Spanish galleon with its swordplay in the latrine. First we had a couple of feelers down at Tom's place, and then went down to the ship. Or I could stop and you'd still go on.

    So starting immediately I'm taking my advice from Delilah on *Lite At Nite*. She really understands me, unlike my optometrist who tends to drop the letters. Generally I bounce upright, radiation streaming through the ozone, warping the sirens and birdcalls, sounding similar to mate but with an "h." The world is briefly silenced, then forgives, all smiles until the adults arrive. I think I see one over there rearranging the cheese plate.
                              A mourning dove sits on the window while we watch the funeral online. That's another kind of hotspot,

as the satellites plot our constant dislocation against a backdrop
of galaxies and those bees that don't sting, unlike the night sticks.
I removed one from my hair, along with an expired license plate
and grape Bubblicious knee-high to the groove. More importantly,
What should I wear to our extinction?

      One day the charger stopped working, yet the sun still feels
warm on my skin. I looted the cracker drawer before leaving on a train,
you on a jet plane, the necklace falling delicately across your neck.
I know how hard it can be to sit quietly, but the real action is on Twitter,
and I only use math to figure out the tip. Get in touch with your boss.
I can't be more explicit, but it's not impossible to undo the chassis,
each wheel the start of something new

                                      after a national anthem sung
to the tune of a dull ache, of lessons learned, when mostly what I hear
is grinding metal and the squeal of your new sneakers on wood floors.
It's time for lunch at the diner that's going to force me to make
a career change, which must be why the lifeguards are clearing the pool,
and not because of that suspicious floating object. In other words,
keep the playbill away from the stage. Somebody new is always trending.

      I've never quite located the dry dock, but all the kids love
Davy Jones. I reset the pedometer to zero when you couldn't get out
of bed, each day with its set of little heartbreaks, and the big one
tucked underneath. Let's have a beer after our run, the clouds piling
like molars in the mouths of celebrities wearing crisply fitted slacks.
Be careful not to let the hair dye stain your skin—I see it lining
the skull. I'm telling this

                            in a letter, and the egrets are mysteriously
disappearing because they don't like living alone. Who can blame them
in the petro burn? It's more than enough loss for one lifetime. Later,
I drove out to the refinery to see the lights architectonic against the night
and the battery slow in the watch, while you changed the station or picked
a different song from the playlist. Best to leave outboard motor repairs
to the professionals.

Does Frisbee count as a sport? Call me Dr. Rockwell.
We surface for air like those giants of the deep, then ask to eat some
of your fries. I will never own a leaf blower, but I've waved one
at the trees; and I've filled out all the proper forms, so tell me why
I still feel sad. There's a towel drying from your trip to the beach
where I bumped my head on a doorframe and you got hit with
a dirty balloon while checking

                                       Instagram on your phone. The wind
took over from there. No one accepted blame for the oil spill upriver,
while I had trouble finding the jar of Vaseline. I've been made available
to take further questions. Let's start with, Where did the leftovers go?
The recording devices are being recorded, and this includes what
you see. My address book is filling up with the dead, but that won't
stop me from skipping a visit to a veterinarian in the heartland.

     A true story is a bit of an oxymoron, though that's the least
of this poem's worries. For one thing, it can't find its keys. It's not
that I'm hidden, but the language buries us. The cat is literally out
of the bag, warm fur with tiny streams of breath through its nose,
or that's what it looks like on the page I've got minimized at work
until my boss steps out for lunch and acupuncture. Me? I prefer
retail therapy at Kmart,

                        big plastic bags swinging from my arms.
Uh, oh, Adderall. It's the cheap drinks that do the most damage,
which is why I never stare directly at the sun. Everything else
is just a quick flare, or that's my personal opinion while stalled out
on the tracks. Actually, it's kind of amazing we survived this long,
waving huckleberries at a grizzly with no interest in spooning,
my head a honeycomb in the shipping lanes.

     Strange days. I'm writing another message on my phone.
Eventually the sugar wore off, so we replenish with pine cones
and needles dropped from a tree we climbed to see our other options
on sweatshirt-and-shorts day, because this seat won't recline in coach.
Anything to squeeze in another iamb, one more box of tinsel to dump
on dad. Lol. Let's face it, cheese can be overrated. We're three sheets

to the wind. I'll take Fred Flintstone
                                            in a paddleboat race. Trade school
is looking better and better because inevitably the stuffing pokes through
the taxidermied surface. That's why I'm down with the quilting bee,
moving in one day and then never moving out, as drive-by shootings
became more frequent when everyone lives in their cars, except for
the satellite pilots we wave at from Earth while watching the final
bird migration perform a barrel roll down the coast.

      The night is a given, though it's not always this full of noise.
My friends shine brightly, so please don't turn out the lights right now,
which isn't the same as a slow fade or rain splashing on the stones.
We carry the remainder in our hands, and things that can be considered
kindling include most of the items in this room. Yours looks nice
in those photographs you posted until the eviction notice. The rest
I can buy with a few swipes
                                  as we work to overthrow the Anthropocene
and its chattering teeth toy we stick our fingers into, pretending they're
fish sticks or evening wear for an entire species. The ski lodge didn't stand
a chance against an avalanche, while our breathing hole is the size of a fist.
I don't want to get over you. Audio out is also audio in. Glitchy. Reverb
is to be human, while twenty dollars should get you dinner at the drum circle
or a scrap of dirty upholstery.

      We couldn't be any hungrier except for the hunger following that,
loosening the sidearm from a holster nervously thrummed. It's spring
in the Southern Cone. I can't fit enough words into the spaces where you were.
Instead, it's glass, steel, and concrete, the patience at the butcher, everything
pushed toward consumption. I once ate a stick of margarine I stole from
the store, then erased most of our texts discussing the Humpty Dance,
though perhaps not in that order.
                                      From what I can see, the plan is to conquer
via one drooping eyelid at a time, each used car swung across the junkyard
by a giant magnet. I'll be making my escape on the rowing machine as you
undo the screws and the coastline sinks underwater. That's what it feels like
when you tap at my grave with a shovel as the green leaves spin, each one

flickering before blinking out. I just watched a Vine of a baby tumbling into a laundry basket. I just watched a Vine of an anaconda swallowing a lion.

    That'll scatter birds from the carcass, wings momentarily darkening the sky in a shriek. Or maybe it's Gilligan after the shipwreck improvising shelter and telling Thurston Howell III to build his own fucking hut. I just need a touch up on my roots. So where does it hurt? Right there where the thinky starts. Who turned on the air conditioning in the reptile house? There must be an instruction manual around here on how to chip away at your pedestal with something other
                                            than a shredded toothpick, even if I'm not a category—I'm a change in the season, as a flood left cracked submersibles floating at our door. Don't tase me, bro. I'm always spilling my drink or get nauseous in the backseat while looking out the window, leaving the hula-hoopers in charge until everything starts wobbling below the knees, like spurned crickets merrily chirping away as the garage fills with fumes, except that arsonists tend to work solo.

    Color pinpricks the retina like an aerosol, less an oasis than whatever you deem a cuddle, or else a cheetah in sunglasses selling Cheetos, because how else do children remember? I feel my enthusiasm waning, but the nearest popsicle stand is miles away or next to fracking. Yet it's not fair to raise expectations after mine drifted out with the trash and Millennium Falcon, although I find it ironic that your favorite season is the one when the days slowly shorten
                                            and the trees tighten their hold. Is that too discursive? Then how about another slammed door? I might regret pressing send on this one, though every message eventually reaches the towns built near the river's edge, salt from the bay mixing with inland waters, the way I listen to a clock ticking behind your voice. Speech is chromatic, not chiaroscuro, although I'm feeling partly dark with some dappling—not devotional, just the skid marks.

    My escape velocity is squeezed from a tube. Yours grazes at the hedges, except the route home isn't this one, slack catapults lining the path at an outdoor nursery before October's first frost.

I've been writing this poem since the summer until I felt a twinge
in my left hamstring after stumbling into the first hurdle, saying,
You might slow me down, but you can't stop me, especially when
the refs aren't looking.
                           So why can't I get this stain off my shirt?
I'm hesitant to apply mayonnaise per the website's suggestion,
but I'm starting to get a little desperate as the mirror neurons cloud
and an ashtray spills onto the floor. Clothes feel softer with Downy,
as our gait matches a clubfooted Nixon. The last time I peeked out
the window, the sun was shining; now rain comes through the roof
while I'm in the stands cheering on the nurses.

      The name on the license says McLovin. Nearly a thousand
traders went to jail for the Savings and Loan scandals, and only one
for the financial collapse of 2008. My hands aren't idle, but they start
the devil's work. Do four tater tots constitute an order or a bath toy?
There's a dream of life in my heart, although today might be better
as a broom. I'll start by taking the sag out of the biscuit. I'll try to
embrace what's good.
                           Yet my alarm clock can get kind of moody.
Occasionally I use it as a gravy ladle or feel near the end, and this is no
different, so please pass me a cookie, taking for granted that people
will stay. There's an artist who organizes D&D games with porn stars.
My neck brace attaches to the parachutes, although I still have to feed
the meter after my credit card got declined. Maybe they'll let us out
early since the first fifty customers get a free plastic spoon.

         Even the hills are alive, giving barnacles the float and avoiding
sleep on purpose while knuckle-dragging the ideal. Then there's splatter.
Half the stores at the outdoor mall are empty, except for Mr. Cherry,
plainclothes detective, watching me fill my purse with merchandise.
But I'm my own stupid sleuth, creeping behind the planters after taking
the dog for a walk with a garrulous hippie, saying, *Please, just tell me
what to do*, then poked myself
                                  in the eye with a selfie stick. This is not
my final destination; neither is the press conference hastily arranged

near the flare from an oil well that kept us up all night, orange and red
flicking across the walls, like the law is always around and yet not
really there. Lake of dreams. Lake of sorrow. Lake of time creasing
the landscape where strange things sprout, or like a child I wandered off,
licking my fingers.

    My winter coat is missing a couple buttons and a shave following
the procedure. I'm not sure if my organs are pink. Fish have evolved
past bipedal, which is preferable to bipolar, but everything exists along
a continuum, rolling a suitcase down the street. We imagine a disco
where the lighthouse fell asleep, slumping over the wheel and snagged
in the refraction. Atoms swerve like that too, but they're not drunk. No,
I don't know Jack, but he might
                              be a friend of yours, serving free pizza
and cake to kids in the cafeteria. There are no embedded reporters
in a virtual war. My tribute is given in bananas and a roll of nickels.
One of Sophie's notepads is shaped like a cupcake, but I use it to lean on
the horn at frog crossings. We're all six degrees of separation from
becoming famous or gnawing down to the knuckle. The sun will set
before I'm done, if it hasn't already.

STATE OF THE UNION

Your flat earth makes it easier
for the tanks to roll,
but I've got a few moves myself,
right after I take out this loan.
There's nothing to see but the war,
and for some that's always
been the view.
I make an X with duct tape
while you cross out the eyes.
If it's guilt by association,
then that's pretty much us.

Another storm is rolling through
as the zoo lines up for a sniff
like medals pinned to epaulets
for following orders and all
the things I've got on my mind,
such as the muffins we eat
on our way to the factory
where we make the robots
that will replace us.
I'd be fine with an implant
that eradicates the past,
although we'll still repeat
the same mistakes, starting
with this hole in the heart.

We etch a flag in our mouth
and stand for the dumplings.
Behind every song is a silence
that doesn't make a sound
unlike this dog whistle
that for some reason I can hear
whenever the brakes screech
and I'm a dirty bird.
We got off to a good start,
but faded down the stretch.
One day someone will pull
the sheet over the gurney.
Yet there's no going back—
the thread is through the loom,
even if parts of history
are moving in reverse,
as the wind blows the trash
faster than we can chase it.
Sometimes you need a change
of scenery on the inside,

tossing darts against the kingdom
and imagining a land lost
beneath the sea.

BENT TO THE LINE

It's not a new morning, it's another morning.
My neighbor likes to play music while working
in the yard. I'm just grateful for another hour
of sunlight after we built the prison but not
the keys, cozied up to the warden, escaping
from here to here.

We paint smiley faces on Pop-Tarts for greatness.
I can't read the fine print, but that's okay
since we're already screwed. The film adaptation
comes next, yet things always feel better
at the movies. Just don't reach over the counter—
that's where we keep the cash and guns.

My challenge is to put it into couplets. First,
I gotta get this tooth fixed, then assess
any damage after sneezing on the machines.
Who has an ear for ghosts? Beneath everything
is a crunching sound, and the next thing
to lose is our jobs.

Nickname's Zippy, sir. Go ahead and lower
a curtain on the speaker. I won't miss the moral.
Some crowd control is in your face,
and some is deeply hidden. You might say
the same thing about Sea World, except to me
the whole place smells like blue.

Geese fly north through the valley, but I still worry
about emo. Actually, I worry about you.
What are the daybreak passages? The bell's success
is its emptiness—that's what makes it ring,
as we dream of a life from below, filling
the bowl with Chex Mix for the party.

The treatment of monuments is to destroy them,
lining up palm trees past the horizon.
I can sit still for almost twenty minutes, except
when you're around. Then it's whatever is good
for the gander. My heart a spitting image.
Poetry sometimes says what it means.

FLUSHING THE LUNGS

We sign up to get lots of free stuff,
but still have to pay each day.
We'd mow the lawn if we had one,
but still have to duck the blades.
I etched my name into the soup
and its greasy film coating
every surface. That must be why I hate
fine dining, and change the channel
whenever golf's on. I've tried to build
as much as I've wrecked, although
late at night I sometimes wonder.

It's not a metaphor, it's an image,
as we watch through the pixels
collecting their own form of dust
next to Walt Disney's head in a freezer.
I only want to be revived if it
involves Alpine Breeze body wash

and a suture, the whoosh of traffic
in the distance. How many houses
will I never see again? I meant
to tell you about the dog, the lead
streaming through the pipes.

After all that history, it's come back
to the battle over water and land.
Soon enough, I'll be on the move
amid crumbling towers and floods.
For now, we collect snow in our
shopping carts, rattling down the street
while the bills go out automatically.
Call me an oversharer, yet you
accumulate a little from every person,
every kitchen table, every crowd.

SNAP TO GRID

Cooler heads may prevail, except the planet
is heating up, while I glance down at my phone
for the text you haven't sent. I'd nickname you
the Kissing Bandit even though we never got
to first base. The cemetery is filled with plastic
flowers, yet we're all part of fallen stars.
Leaving the lights on won't keep away
the creep. If only the good people knew.

Sadness is a quilt in the late afternoon,
or maybe I just miss you too much—
the nearness of world to weave.
When did it begin with so many rules?
So much for catch and release, for waking up
early. Words are crutches for the tongue

or a flotation device meant for the pool
that gets taken to a deep-sea rescue.

The shelves were empty before the storm,
but I was elected the green grocer watching
the planes fly over. We still have to feed
the sky in a desert everywhere you look.
I read an advertisement for an advertisement
in last month's copy of *Auto Trader*
as the clutch slips its vroom, like sweaty boys
who grapple during gym class.

Yet occasionally we skid free, a small patch
of sun in the darkest times until we pull
the curtains. Your cat rubs against my shins
as if it really likes me, then sends pictures
of bird heads in a spreadsheet. It's still easier
to swim with flippers trademarked Dudley Doolittle,
even if there's really no escape.
This country is a gun-toting nightmare.

THE PASSENGER

I dropped my phone in the ocean,
        and now the fish play Candy Crush,
clanging hearts down there in the dark.
        Life is short and brutish,
especially when my parents ground me
        because we're all going to die one day,
and some of us sooner than others.
        Sunlight ripples across the window pane,
momentarily blinding the parakeet,
        though not its tiny song.

Every page is filled with words
        with letters like little teeth,
or maybe it's a briefcase.
        Yet it won't hide the tear in the fabric
or disguise the worry behind the paycheck.
        We refill the prescription along the way
and pick up the dog from the kennel
        where we usually know what to do,
nose pressed to the fence.
        So many species will survive us.

We ate a basketful of eggs,
        then made the bed
after waking up to countless emails,
    videos of squirrels sipping soda,
and a child's xylophone version
        of "Home on the Range"
or "People Make the World Go Round."
        When did life become mostly wasting time?
I keep waiting for things to get better,
        though sometimes the goal is just to finish.

Whose friend are you?
    —Friend of the firefly.
Most of what we tried to fix ended up broken,
    including the handlebars on a moped,
so now I deliver food with a drone
        cooled with wet rags and a squirt gun
while the police keep circling the block.
    An indoor ice rink started to melt in the heatwave,
as did the meat in our fridge,
        slowing down the bend of hurt toward healing.

We are so far from a culture of love
    it can be hard to even imagine.
There's not a cake to be made from it,

    no sun for the rose;
at least that's how it feels to the new kid
    and the leftovers for the garbage.
I've seen pets eat better.
    Until then, I'll be the swivel to your stick,
driving cross country with its rows of corn
    and memorials to the massacres.

CODE SWITCH

I launched a satellite from the bedroom window
                              and its view
    of a parking lot and yellowing wet wipes.
We accidentally kick the dog bowl
                    under the fridge
    the same way we press down on the keys.
                                  Catch you later,
    except there isn't one,
                    not even the chance to say no,
as thunder echoes down the alley,
                        rolling like something broken
    called the system.

But I'm grateful for moments of hope,
                    the sun returning
    after a long winter,
               its blinding strobe light flashing
on the smokestacks by the river
              where we cleaned up
    needles in the mud.
Let's plan a trip to the candy shop. You can get there
                          via Cricket Lane
    while walking the dog
                  and tossing hay to the horses

      by the armful
                as they gather at the hedges.

It's like a menagerie around here,
                including you and me,
    except we've got better tools and less training,
                    like the time
I drove a forklift into a pyramid of paper towels
                    or you miss
      a bucket with the compost.
That's why we need to get focused,
                so please pass the Adderall.
The haircut took five minutes,
          but it was good to lose the bulk.
Next is shaving the epaulets,
        before giving the moist parts
    some talcum.

A cloud of bumblebees moved through
                a freshly plowed field,
    sucking a sweetness from the air,
                  as we try to get rid of the bosses
      and I fumble with the shutter.
The work goes late into the night,
              then we meet the dawn in sequins.
How to document a day? I signed a contract
                to sign another contract
      spilling over the page,
like a tugboat stranded on a sand dune,
              like a birdsong in the basement.

SWARM

I hit refresh, but it doesn't do any good;
sometimes you just need to start over.
We pay our tribute to the king in bales of hay
stolen from his fields.
Snowflakes gently swirl
around a tree's bare branches,
but I'll be gone by summer,
a pile of shredded newspapers left by the door
after we lugged our house up the hill
with the chickens coming home to roost.

Call it plainsong or lament
with the lungs removed
or a broken bottle pressed to the throat
after I disabled my email,
although now I won't know
when to show up drunk for your wedding.
Every car honked along a mile stretch of road
until the school bus turned off its lights,
because we love the children
except when we don't.

This part's not for posterity.
The train has one wheel off the track,
and worry makes the language constrict,
just as some knots take years to untie
or to escape the bullhorn in your ear.
I can only write this when I'm sitting still,
yet work is the jailer of words
like starfish slow to scatter
or how we end up a little bit like our parents.
One of mine started drinking at 5 a.m.

Dumb bunny getting trapped near that.
The light flickers in its spectrum from blue to black.
Each stop sign conceals a go,
though that's not why our head hurts.
The windows make everything fuzzy like a trumpet,
even if sometimes there's no way to fix it.
I mean, you might win some
but you just lost one,
and I'm not talking about our incisors,
because when long-distance trucking gets automated
who will you talk to late at night?

Instead it's a debit card in a landslide
and an errant glue gun tucked in our waistband
according to the nervous duchess.
Things kind of worked out for a while
but not really,
each piece of glass cracking
in its own unique pattern,
then it cost $50,000 to cap all our teeth.
I used to drive fast; now I take the bus,
and where did I put that ladder?

The sauna may be running out of steam,
but not me—I'm full of it.
A spider floats its web
inside the skeleton's ribs
where we last saw our heart
and its silhouette of a bird.
The universe's moral arc is getting longer,
so wake me up when this press conference
is over, like a backyard pool the kids swim in
filled with dead leaves.

I wouldn't call the fire intentional,
although it quickly spread through the house.
Sometimes you just have to endure,
pulling Saran Wrap from the lettuce.
I've got stories to tell,
but not right now.
The bar at the airport takes us just as far,
while the internet signal constantly drops,
spilling information like leftover Muppets,
as we bail water from the rowboat with a spoon.

A front moves up the seaboard,
which is different from the *Quiet Storm* I listen to
when I get home late
and turn on the lamp that wobbles
for a moment on its base.
Catapults used to surround the moat;
now it's called a drone strike from below the horizon
that's also the top edge of my computer.
I don't count feel; I count Benjamins,
as the Dow goes over 20,000,
yet tile floors are still the coldest.

There's a lot of noise in here
and out there too.
Firetrucks race to the scene,
but the damage is farther away—
just follow the foot soldiers on patrol
and whatever I made for lunch.
I'm trying to reach the river with this clutch
of transmissions as a companion
for the absence that it makes,
filling crevices with jelly and a shotgun wedding.
This, this, this, and this.

What a ragged mess, but at least it's toothpaste
on my shirt this time.
When did the slope start to get so slippery?
My heart blazes with hurt or spicy wings,
and not the flappy kind.
I said I'll see you on the other side,
although I'm not sure there is one—
just two ends of a revolver.
A small frog darts beneath a bush
after we back an exhaust pipe up
to the edge of the forest.

Fighter jets fly over the stadium in formation
while we wave with cotton candy.
They say it's supposed to be spring soon,
but I don't see it,
and there's no getting the cigarette smoke
out of the upholstery.
The signage at the zoo is confusing,
though we should also be on display beneath
the smokestacks and packaging
while we stare at our phones along with the police.

It might be dark earlier now,
yet some day the light will return,
filtering through the beekeeper's mask
while holding an empty can of Coke.
The sun rises over a flat earth doubling
as a dispensary filling the day planner
with pharmaceuticals.
We take our authority with a mountain of salt.
We bury it.
America pulls a white curtain around the surgeon.

HELP WANTED

The heart is a percussion
played on skin and metal,
yet there's a quiet
deep in the blue.
The hills and the buildings
may be quantum,
but the body holds out
for as long as it can,
even after it stops moving,
like the insurance agent
sitting at the kitchen table.
The whole house is crooked
with the bundle of bones
you left behind
the way a bird gathers
twigs for a nest,
except it won't fit in the back
of your car while driving
to buy party supplies.
The children always notice.
My life got buried
somewhere along that route
like walking down
a narrow corridor
with a clown shaking
near the end.
Or so it seemed to me
and the snowplow operator
in August, muttering,
The walls are closing in,
and, *Am I alive on a Sunday?*
during a search for home
that becomes a series
of blank rooms

until you step out
and into the water.

BUSINESS AS USUAL

We circle the block to find the sun
and a parking spot for our heartache
while the birds keep singing
in the trees. I put it on a leash,
but still prefer the stray, even if
there's an anvil in my head
whenever I watch you leave.

They'll practically give away
the TVs but never the dinner.
For that, you'll always have to pay.
The knife is discerning behind
the mic. I lost most of my books
and glued the rest to the floor,
yet I've always dreamed of dunking.

You can call me an artist but only
when I'm washing the dishes.
I don't know what's coming next.
It's both a room freshener
and a body mist, and I can't say
I disagree, considering the troubles
we've had with boundaries.

I don't need any more stuff, although
you can never have too much tinsel.
There's coastline, and then there's
only waves. Sometimes kindness
arrives out of nowhere. You can put

all sorts of things on a waffle,
but that crunch was part of my tooth.

This poem got read at a wedding
of the forest and the fire until my throat
hurt. Rows and rows of conditioner,
yet we still got flakes or willy-nilly.
An expressway also curves through
this room, as the sonar fills with trash
amid the quiet and the noise.

OLD WINE IN NEW BOTTLES

There are a thousand stakes
but just one heart,
so strike behind the mask.
My dinner is beans and heading downhill;
everything else is lipstick on a pig.
Eventually we find the door
that only leads to the bathroom.
We watch open carry in the public square,
the way history writes itself
if you let it.

It also tastes like floorboards,
with a hand on the back of the neck
or a garden withering in the sun.
There's no pretty way to say this,
but it's still a metaphor.
Sometimes you don't want to go home,
though that's no reason to guzzle rosé
during a heatwave.
Art isn't therapy for the state,
so don't let a camel have all the humps.

In other words, let it rip.
First we need a reboot
followed by an expectorant
while how-to leaflets fall from the sky.
The age of Man is over,
as even the stones speak.
I share a sugar cube with a donkey
standing on the roof.
What's a portrait, anyway?
We cross borders every day.

Snapchat isn't fast enough
for what we've seen
or for being alone with our thoughts
as a star chart peels from the ceiling.
Equations are for the doctor,
while we steal the prescription script
and practice the art of refusal.
Rivers might reach the sea,
but not the ones
with all the dams on them.

Welcome back to the desperation.
The speeches call for blood.
My family is like a menagerie
chasing a brown bunny down its hole.
How much scotch to how much soda?
When do you want to meet?
Lots gets left out of the stories,
whether personal or shared.
Mine lost its grip beneath a tractor;
yours remains unfulfilled.

You are what the network produces.
The panting is contagious,
trying to stave off the collapse

that the predators mask
with their scent and mandatory retina scans.
Instead, put a little flavor in my ear.
We climb the trees until they topple,
then eat dinner over the sink,
Golden Arches lined up to the landfill.
No one should let me fly this thing.

LEVITATE THE PENTAGON

1)
I took the remnants to the dumpster
because memory is like that too—
its pain pills crisp as bacon,
otherwise known as the crash and burn.
The rest fogs over in the voting booth
for our choice of ailments,
starting with the good dad.
I don't give up, but I do,
and reset with the leaves.

2)
Gold is just a shiny object,
yet in this world
you still have to pay to play.
I rented an RV, but can't take it
to Canada, so now I mostly mumble
to myself or turn the screw
until it spins. They say
it's funny how things change
while we sit with the skeletons.

3)
I'd watch you leave,
but my head is already emptied.
Rain chased music from the streets,
and a hurt can be larger
than its chronicle.
Must not sleep. Must warn others.
So what else is for sale? ¯_(ツ)_/¯
There's more hope on the outside,
except a drone stole my hoverboard.

4)
The inmates may have taken over
the asylum, except they're not inmates,
and it's not an asylum.
There are neurons surrounding the heart.
Grades aren't due,
but I'm hardly passing,
though I know how to spread sand
on the snow. The test consists of
keeping busy and listening
for what falls between the cracks.

LISTENING IN

Even the clouds are mechanical floating offshore
on a server where the whales bump into them
and jellyfish glow green in the moonbeams.
I'm an algorithm feeder with a pain in my jaw.
Another day without you is sweater weather.

The world's richest 1% took 82% of the wealth
generated in 2017. I probably owe part of that
on my credit card. The grocery store meat is sealed
in plastic, just as sometimes it can be hard to let go,
including the immaterial and the stars.

What's the attrition rate for swimmers? The sky
comes down on top of me. The sand blows over
the wall. Time is at its most deadly when it's quietest,
patiently collecting cans on the side of the highway
and stepping on my headphones.

It might seem like an ending, except we're always
in the middle. I still went back to the hotel room
for a nap. That'll teach me not to stay out late drinking
with a job interview in the morning for a position
to swap out the stop signs or have a sandwich with you.

Hello, it's the Martian. The signals are mostly digital.
Each letter is a tool. But the woods make us restless,
a bundle of memory and impulses, like red velvet cake
seen in a delirium after I volunteered for the dunk tank
and hayride. I still can't get it straight.

INVISIBLE SCRIPT

Whole worlds on fire.

A black ship in a red sky.

I'd rather walk, but I don't know the way.

The hungrier we get, the longer the line.

No page is ever empty.

We sign it—Forgotten.

One note at a time, throwing out the bugle.

The crush of it all beneath the sound stage.

Parasites line our intestines.

The things we do for love.

The rest of the time we're alone.

EVERYBODY IN MY FEED

We play the piano while crouched beneath it,
its belly threatening to crush us
like my grandmother's wisdom and Canadian Club
or my truck is bigger than your truck.
I still confuse fact and fiction,
though not as much when it's cold.
We decorate scarcity and compare it to children
briefly running free in the streets,
because heaven is a place called earth
except when it's not.

No wonder we need a little uplift,
a pat on the back when times are bad,
like the rocket that took those guys to the moon
or maybe banana bread and a breath mint
after breaking into the zoo
where the lions ate the La-Z-Boy Recliner
that smelled of sweaty leather.
We followed that with a retinal scan,
and now I'm in the database
with the other fools for love.

But I'm grateful to wake up next to you,
even if it's only once a week.
I'm the crackle to your pop,
or the things you give your life to like a stowaway.
That must be why my nickname is Below Deck.
Either way, we use the stove for heating
when the road stretches for miles,
with a detour through the conference hotel
where someone tried to sell us a pillow
after all the talks and speeches.

It was hard to choose at the vending machine
that we found in the middle of a desert.
Its candy bar was shipped via Amazon Prime
and the nosebleed we got while weeping
for the vanished forest behind our house.
That's where the owls soared in the dark
with mice gripped tight between their talons
and hearts rapidly beating,
because the gatekeepers want to be wooed.
Our clean clothes are pretty filthy.

I got a tattoo of a person getting a tattoo
or maybe it was my mom in the distance
calling me to dinner.
I'd walk away from it all if I could,
like a spider lost in its web
or maybe in your daydreams.
If you take me to your leader,
we'll end up at the dump
where new shoots poke through a scorched earth
after the bugs survive us.

You smeared butter on the camera's lens
to give it a soft focus.
I have no idea what comes next,

but I'm still trying to fix it.
That's around the time I heard someone say,
Just set out his bowl, although
I might have been mistaken.
No god or celebrity will save us—
only the children from the future,
if they make it that far.

I hear a sputter in the static
as the transmission comes through.
This poem gathers the scraps
that the leaf blower missed,
or else it's a walking stick
for an inverted mountain in winter.
But I'm glad we've made it this far
with the rain on the side of your face
on our quest to find warm donuts
and never being able to predict someone's mood.

Those childhood memories are like a juicer
or a dude in a gorilla suit.
How much money do the rich really need?
I bruised my lip on the gift bag.
The shape of the machine
is the shape of its connections,
and some doctors have more patients
than they can deal with.
Even the penguins are anxious about the rising seas
that we watched on computers at the office.

One of my favorite phrases is, *Stay in your lane*;
yours is, *I'll be in touch*.
We try breathing underwater,
but it won't rinse the stain.
A thousand miles above is only empty space
or a UFO tucked behind a comet.

You can't wait around for hope to take over,
which is more than I can say for this circling bat
or the peace we try to imagine.
Thank you for ignoring that email.

The RAV4 was last year's best-selling car.
You got a rip in your favorite sweater
while making a small catapult for the meatballs.
It's better than going to the dentist when your teeth hurt
from too much smiling and *Yes, more, please.*
That didn't stop you
from aimlessly wandering the streets,
with a lighthouse in the distance
leading to the low-slung cliffs
blurred by a foggy window.

I just like the sound of the word pony,
though there are a thousand distractions from the mic.
I had to set up an account to set up an account,
then share my location with the police,
except you already knew that,
as the cruise ship starts to take on water,
and all I've got is a mop.
I never should have sold those jet skis,
but I needed the money for a class on coding
at the local community college.

A blimp wobbles low in the sky
above a sold-out Rose Bowl show.
We'd rather be hunter-gatherers
with our black backpacks and hooded sweatshirts
slowly going extinct.
The garden center doesn't do much business in a blizzard
after leaving the bodies on Everest.
No wonder all the words sound like nouns.

It's the revenge of the animal on your unbuttoned shirt,
beef jerky stuck to your molars.

Later, I rolled up my sleeve for the needle,
asking, *Where did everybody go?*
It's just me and whatever Miley Cyrus is now.
I'd send you a letter except I don't have your address.
I'll take the dark net instead.
One day this body will be mostly compost,
so please find me when you're finished.
I'll be sitting here in the silence
except for all those words
and the endless clatter of dishes piled in the sink.

I found the end of the song by a river
where heavy cattails thump the banks.
I found the end of the song in your heart
where a swan mates with a Roomba.
Too much memory isn't always a good thing,
with its crayon for stubby fingers.
Instead we listen to the noise
and its sound of a broken compass
as the sun dips below the horizon
like swallowing a lollipop.

You sat on the plastic bag with my sandwich in it
after I said I'm tired of hearing about beauty.
I'd take a paddleboat to the store in a storm
if I had one, or something more
than bad credit and a personal loan
for the ring you lost in Oklahoma,
probably drunk again at a rest stop.
I filled up another page like a kid might.
I listened to the night
and its ghost in every poem.

SO MUCH PARADE

Chicken tenders or cordon bleu—
it's all the same to me.

What makes sense is oppressive,
but what doesn't is brutal.

Here's to getting up earlier;
I'll see you in the nighttime.

The buds go from yellow to green,
except your realism isn't mine.

I want a clock that doesn't tick
so that I'm not constantly starting over.

That's not a mashup, that's a trash truck
in the parking garage beneath the mall.

To faster and more we add static,
but I like to look through the donut hole.

That's why they're called baked goods,
though where I live, pot is still illegal.

I've always been restless,
siccing a cat on the bird song.

Isn't the heart already under water?
All that garbage is on its way to the sea.

GOING OFF SCRIPT

I sent a friend request to the sunset.
I wish I could take away the flood.
Instead, we tug at the necktie like a leash
or a crack at the base of the wall,
jackhammers at the ready
as the day slips away.
It would be more fun if we didn't go to work.
The words blow in with the exhaust,
while other times you sit and stare,
rubbing out the stars with your knuckles,
also known as paw paws or everything singed.
That's one way to find a groove,
as shadows fill the valley split by a languid river
and the bubbles of industrial runoff
where a heron tentatively dips a skinny leg
and the big green frogs scatter.
You've been gone so long,
yet it was only yesterday.
That strange, tingling feeling is either life
or my spidey-sense. In any case,
I haven't gotten enough of it,
as the economy sucks your blood
until the nurse finds another vein
or reinforces the ceiling with clown-paint seepage.

We're easily distracted, composing the email
before it's sent, like suds to water at the car wash.
One theory is that extraterrestrials
are breeding us for food,
but like you, I have my own hungers,
and I paid my bill over the phone,
though not the bill after that
after failing to match the illness with its treatment.
Our DNA got all over everything,

especially the crock pot and donkey,
even though the authorities had already found us.
We fold napkins at the group house,
yet they still end up on the floor
next to the optometrist's dented eye chart.
No one has ever treated me better,
except for that nun at school with a ruler
teaching poetry as rote.
Let the kids play, I chanted,
refusing to give up,
despite the long line to the bathroom
and the show already started.
I couldn't miss it if I wanted to,
and I'm not talking about the eclipse,
because even a plumber can blot out the light.

It's one hook per carcass at the slaughterhouse,
while the generals use bombs on the rest.
The heads of Confederates tumble
from their plinths. The rot starts
at the roots, thin as hair,
spreading its way through the leaves,
while the slide curves upward for a few.
I'd love to go on vacation,
except I forgot my credit card at the gas station
next to a bag of nuts.
Home was in the end.
That must be why it's called a jumpsuit—
one piece from all the parts.
You wear your heart on your sleeve,
but then it gets cold,
and you put a jacket over it.
I'd say it's time to get serious,
except we're already weeping.
The flag planted on our skulls
always flies at half-mast

next to a plastic bucket labeled TIME
in block letters and a toy windmill
wobbling in the breeze.

ATTENTION SPAN

Plastic trophies gleam in rows
like the many ways dogs go woof.
Sometimes sound travels faster than light
when there's a rumbling in the distance.

The birds only sing after the rain stops.
I bought a painting of a cake instead of the real thing.
Flares don't go far in the fog,
including the one inside me.

Each night we wonder at the end of the pier.
The screen door keeps out most of the bugs.
I set up a small hospital at the truck stop,
but one day I'll be tired of all the pain.

Grates in the road keep the cattle from crossing.
Brass instruments warp in the heat.
This is my song, though.
Everyone follows the ghosts.

MORE BANG FOR THE BUCK

It's getting a little loud in here
and also outside my head.
Valentine's Day was a storm of Tex-Mex
or proper nouns. Tickle me, Elmo?

That bird is back. The elevator repair
service showed up a few hours later,
though I don't know if we're going
up or down. Power speaks to specters,
smells like embers. But I should
have played by the rules more
instead of joining the Dumb Dumb Club
for one.

Still, it feels good to be back
if by that you mean interplanetary.
Each brain may fire differently,
except now you're just scaring
that child. The wildlife needs room
to roam after making due
with the dulcet, because every poet
is already dead. I don't know
why; it's what the rototiller told me—
the one you placed in the basement
next to the pruning shears
and gift wrap.

I meant tuning fork, but each
Fast and Furious is more successful
than the last. We crush on them
hard for humble, then wear me
like a spigot, yet I'd give it up
for good. For now, I'm shaking
and baking, and we're sore from all
that coffee, though I will never
bend my back to bow. That's not
the same as claustrophobia,
but it's close, less afraid
of what's lost than what remains.

A NEW HOPE

The rain patters like it's taking a walk,
    except I'm all wet
                        no matter what the weather.
My dream song chews on aluminum foil,
    but chokes on flu shots
                        at the office.
Money doesn't want to help the sick
    because it's another kind of disease.
Just don't leave me with the fiber   favor   father.
They say the best jobs are at the fulfillment center
        following robots around,
    yet where's the reason in things?
I paint the tree leaves green
                            to cover up the scarring,
    as the lights flicker off
                        in the middle of a tunnel.
The narratives entrap us,
    though we still have so many emails to send,
                so many wounds to suture
    beneath a slow leak in the ceiling
where the disco love globe used to spin.

We made two meals for $5
                              and left the dishes in the sink
    like the lookout tower on Sourdough Mountain
    because only you can prevent forest fires
unless, of course,
                you can't.
I know the feeling.
There are also medals for being bad,
    and hair in the drain is the least
                            of our worries.
We looked for a little quiet and an empty room,

    only to end up asking:
                                  Where did everybody go?
I took the Bigfoot costume to the laundry
       with sweaty sick-bed sheets,
    avoiding the cops and paparazzi,
but not the ice-cream-truck jingle on repeat   and OCD.
When the world feels like it's getting faster,
       I remember how you pass the gravy—
    for that I might have to wait for hours.
Maybe that's why the novel is a good form
                                     for telling stories.

The dolphins don't care about us,
       but we've got an opinion
                            on almost everything,
    including a bet on the over/under
       after making wildly bad decisions.
Some take years to dig out from,
       while others follow you around like a dog
    mistaking a firefly
                     for a dumpster.
That's why I cook barbeque with more
    lighter fluid than coals,
                          because it makes
       the signs shine brighter.
A wheelchair silently rolls across the linoleum,
    and you can't put your hand up to stop it.
The last time I felt such a disturbance
                              in the Force,
       I was at Benihana surrounded
    by spilled drinks   and bent steak knives.
An alarm clock above the bar keeps
                              a different time.
Even back then
          I didn't want to go home.

CONTRAPUNTAL

Wool in the winter.   A tarp on the ground.

A cold sunlight floods the room.

We are an empire of dirty socks,
    of the morning starting without us.

Mismatched caps on the dried-out markers.

One day we'll be the future farmers,
    although now we just dig ditches.

    *

It's your thirsty bin.   A tilted paper cup.

The self is transitional.   My fake moustache,
    for instance.   Your wooden leg.

The kid is trying to go fast on a bicycle.

Paint can also be applied with a knife.

I'll take the cheap one, as machines
    fulfill our order.

    *

Some people come back and some don't.

It's a small town so all the cops know me.

The pool was drained decades ago,
    its low echoes surrounded by scrub.
I am found ghost.   Shadows cast by the gate.

I pound my fist on the PlayStation
    after losing another life.

    *

You clear a path with a bulldozer
    or napkin.   My spirit lost at sea.

A satellite dish on every terrace.

The chronology might be wrong,
    yet time still moves ahead.

When does the bandage pull off of that?

Stinging the eyes like a wedding song.

THE DOLLAR AND THE JUGULAR

They put the defibrillator in a pill, but it still won't heal
our hearts. I made it as far as the middle of the line
after playing croquet in a hospital parking lot tracking
every flight to nowhere, because it's hard to get
out of bed without a little bit of hope. I know that
from the messenger; I heard it in the leaves, clanging
like a buoy outside the harbor. The dog needs a walk
and probably a bath, but I've seen people treat their pets
better than humans, even if I share most of my DNA
with monkeys given peanuts for completing basic tasks.
Mine involves spraying air freshener in the bathroom;
yours for adding the appropriately colored food dye.
I might be smiling on the outside, but this Percocet
is making it worse after they polluted the water and took
the jobs away, then bulldozed the house with an ambulance.

Our fathers were wounded in the war, though that doesn't
mean I need to read it—you deal with it and move on,
while tap, tap, tapping out a beat as the map rolls back
on itself like all camels have one or two humps. My humps.
I used my savings plugging up a lifeboat called Jarvik,
but I wouldn't drink the water from the Charles where
we found Tom Brady's cell phone bobbing. Another parent
jumped in to retrieve it, muttering, *So many kids*.
I was distracted by my plastic visor softening in the sun,
because I may have started it, but I can't control it
after kicking bullies in the shins before going over the wall.
There's a web connecting everything, and a mammal
only wants to be quiet and warm. That's small comfort
when the mud starts to freeze and the tidal pool at the zoo
is our original home.

We loosened the belt a notch with each mozzarella stick—
or at least I did—and it was totally worth it. Sometimes I can't
say no, but I'll generally pipe down for a treat. The sewage
backed up into the river where it mixed with industrial runoff,
and even the birds are failing. That's not emo, as generations
pass down their defeat. Obey the little rules and break
the big ones. We film the police while they film us during
a symphony of car alarms, of candy kept under glass
behind the counter. The warbler is how it sounds, or wedged
in a snowbank as the light starts to fade and everyone crowds
the fire escape. The bookmarks are cute, as we grind through
the mouth guard while awake and sweep up the fragments
or dolls with colored marbles for eyes completely oblivious
to Valentine's Day and satellites watching you except for
the soggy ecosystem under the porch.

It feels strange to sit through a commercial, like what
the bat knows when it's drifting off to sleep. On the Platte,
the sand cranes make a beautiful thrum in the cooling dusk,
yet the best this will be is a stutter when we're choking

on injustice. I folded your clothes clean from the laundry,
with the music in a minor key and winter lingering.
After so many fire drills, we started to ignore them,
as a searchlight scans a darkening sky. Actually, it's an ad
for a club in the suburbs or maybe a new Chili's.
Either way, I'm ready to have a good time, because the sun
will come out tomorrow unless it doesn't. Scuba divers
put a boot on our car after we drove it into the lake.
That's where everything goes, you said, while standing
in line at the dessert bar, a fleet of armed drones hovering
at the entrance.

The world may be getting smaller, but the itch is still hard
to scratch. Someone buried a pistol in the garden after too much
standing around and talking, then Googled: How many sharks
are there in the ocean? It came back with a weather report
that made me grab my galoshes and an eye patch, gladly walking
the plank for your love and its biscuit nuzzle all lazy and flaky.
That's why I'm writing a memoir on addiction. Some days
you literally hit a wall, but when the truck went over the side
of the bridge, it made another one, arcing through the night.
Hide from the men. My ringtone is a fox in the woods.
You called it aura, I said ambience—the low hum of body
meeting machine, of the army waiting in formation.
Remember when we were kids and rode around on bikes?
Mine was a tan 10-speed with a southwestern paint scheme
that's now crushed in a landfill, and goodbye to that.

We leave the piano out of tune and push it against the window,
then stopped to watch the trees slowly blossom and skywriters
surrender to the clouds. There's always cereal for dinner
and flip flops for the Presidential Physical Fitness Test.
How long until the police arrive? There's one sitting right there
at the corner. I can see both the freeway and the railroad tracks
from my window, but I've never been so far from home.
Eventually you get used to it, the shadow on the page,

as this mood lighting is the worst, and why does lavender
seem like the dead's favorite smell? It can be hard to find
an exit, the seas choking with jellyfish amid the acids
and trash, while so much of what we imagined ended up
on the cutting-room floor that we came to be known
as post-scissors, playing scratch-offs with a pulled tooth.
Just make sure to flush when you're done.

I'm not going to work today, and I might not go tomorrow,
either. It's been dumb months, and some of it hungover
after wiping up with muffins. I was gonna eat those,
but now it's too late, and the floor is covered in crumbs,
like when we spilled beer on the picnic tables that the raccoons
later came and licked. After the drought comes the flood.
Poetry isn't quite certain, with its roof open to the blue,
yet here I am on the third floor where we topple ourselves
from the throne and thick rugs. But because our phones
were off, nobody noticed. Sometimes it's the doctor
who kills you, although you're bad medicine now.
We're careening, which isn't the same as things going badly,
except that we'll refuse to admit defeat and collect
used toothbrushes, every mouth a unique shape flaring up
in the savannah sun.

The farm equipment isn't ours, so we borrowed it
for the night, harvesting a barren earth's dreams after
the human. Then it's back to the kitchen lowering a basket
into the fryer, sending endless emails, ready for a drink.
You don't give a parakeet a haircut; you clip its wings.
But the mother needs to get better. All the pain that came
and went. Either way, memory can be heavy, its sandbag
leaking water and a low sky. Here's a salute to the stoners.
We leave a mirror in the woods, shiny among the leaves,
but the other animals ignore it, less restless than us
after our hands got tangled in the fence or running fists
through our hair. That's where you found me, watching

laundry tumble in the dryer while scrolling through
my phone. Early morning light, I missed you. I'll catch you
at the end of this night.

The pigeon is oblivious while pecking at a trash bag
and sipping neon from a tube. Feeling the creep,
we twist in the sheets and get low enough to capture
tadpole substitutes for fish sticks after depleting seas
that swallow coastal cities as the dying are given candy
to suck. I wrapped it in a shawl, seeking relief from
the leeches, including these endless ATM fees.
The medical cot stretches all the way to the margins,
scraping the floor as it goes, then knocking at the door.
No more angels. We're the outtakes, so no wonder
narrative bores us; we prefer a swarm of honeybees
above a blue lake with clouds reflected on its surface.
Sorrow, I see you following; and while I'm not an optimist,
I have a bit of hope, which confuses them, and sometimes us,
like whatever you're doing under that blanket.

But if that's what you call lovin', then I'll take two scoops,
because a hand on the knee is better than a fist in the face,
although sometimes they're the same. The water in my building
was brown today, so now I need a pass to go the bathroom.
That's okay, since I'd keep an eye on me too. We're likely
to ghost. The only thing I took to the desert was a spoon
for scooping contrails out of the sky or to get my head
erased where big engines rev in the night. The rest
is a distraction when loss becomes contagious, imagining
the airport from a distance, your clothes like a bullet,
knowing that everything goes away in the end. Politics might be
apocryphal, yet it has real effects, as an oven does to butter.
History provides perspective, including how brutal most
of it has been. Then what happened? I'm sure it involved
going to work, our language sore like a throat.

LOOSE CANNON

I tried to feed a whale a Triscuit,
    but that's no reason to call the law.
Besides, we were in international waters
    with lots of squid and bobbing plastic
    like the sun and her flowers.
I took a sip with a straw,
    yet was as wet as the termite is to the wood.
I'm good at that as well as not getting up.
I could eat a burrito for every dinner,
    then play fetch until exhausted,
    as a firetruck rushes around in circles,
    while the drought is already inside.
The cameras follow us everywhere.

We wake to tanks rolling through the streets
    and the president in fatigues
    watching a parade of middle fingers.
The rest is a distraction or worse.
This country is rotten to its core,
    treats need like a bucket to kick.
No more bar soap. No more 4th of July.
I'm not sure what's certain any more
    except that the cat doesn't like it
    when you rub its fur that way.
So don't put the cap on the backyard telescope
    when we're all low beneath the stars,
    beer sloshing from a plastic cup
    and onto our Adidas.
That last honk was the loudest one.
Time flows like a blanket slowly smothering each life.
No wonder we're so patient,
    telling the ghosts not to worry,
    but someone had to go ahead and fire that gun.

Now it's duck and cover
    behind the Starbucks counter,
        my name misspelled on the spinning cup.
That's okay, because I'm adopted,
    and there aren't enough lifeboats for this ship,
    which must be why you're always
    hanging around the porthole.
Good riddance, you said, wiping
    your greasy hands on the back of your khakis.

TROUBLE IN MIND

The shadows deepen in their blue
                            synonymous with summer,
    as we watched it on screen.
One day you're there,
               and the next you're not,
    or maybe it's called the kennel.
That's when we get a little pouty
                        after leaving the putt just short
    of the clown's mouth,
                like a truth spoken to power.

We work toward the good,
                    which is harder than it looks.
Big banks take the little ones.
I've been to Chickamauga
                and Winnemucca too,
    gleaming with neon, guns, and Denny's.
There's a time for silence
                and a time to speak,
but beneath it all
        is a tremor.

The trees are at their fullest bloom
                                  right outside the window
        except for the ones
                  that didn't survive the winter
          along with part of you.
Put the rest on hangars in the closet,
                              the way poetry
        goes off script,
                  trying to hold our heads
above the water.

You can't comb the weather,
                            but you can rent a beach,
        placing one word
                  next to another.
Nightmares are more visceral than dreams,
                                    yet some children play
        in the streets without worry.
At the optometrist I can't see a thing,
                          except for low fireworks
        in the rain.

There's a music to everything,
                          even if it mostly sounds
        like noise.
Narrative is no less complicated,
                            especially when the detectives
        pull a body from the lake,
                          its next biography yet to be written.
Your other name is possession,
                        the knot slipping free
        from the weave.

ONE DAY AT A TIME

We ate dinner at a diner in New Jersey coming back from the game where you sat on my sunglasses while thumbing through old photos on your phone. We spoke the language of pork chops and soda until I lost you at the crossing—the movie version stars lots of orphans. One house has vinyl siding; another is made of stone. Either way, smoke pours under the door. Yet the deepest night is made from dreams and the fire alarm of the present that fits under my hat when secured by a chinstrap and a trash bag wrapped around it.

The hotel pool is a little murky but the goggles help with that or only dipping your toe in—I don't judge. This is a record of more than me on the waitlist, stirring syrup into creamed corn after machines seeded the clouds, bringing more rain. That's why this evening is my own little storm surge, overflowing the docks. It's also known as picking up the pieces on a trip to the skyway, since it's always quieter after we exit the streets or try to hit the high notes when there's all that junk piled above my head.

The grass grows greener in the lengthening shadows next to lead lining the pipes. I couldn't take it anymore, but I still did. You said that's life, yet to me it feels closer to death and its relentless sprawl, its lowered boom mic we squeak into. The rooftops stop at the water and a row of police cars where I sent you a quick Snap that cuts off my head like the kings of France and England, because the messages have to come from somewhere, spilling their tails like a comet or maybe directions shouted from the back seat as the history gets erased with each click.

I'll take my succor one sugar cube at a time while waiting for a pump at the gas station and hoping that you'll text from beneath a purple sky so astounding it almost seemed real, which isn't exactly the same as too good to be true. There's a difference between the peach you buy and the peach you eat, but you said to burn it all down, and I couldn't completely disagree. We touch both hearts and lungs in the hospital

for pneumonia where the nurses get nervous watching the continent
of plastic expand.

Thanks for noticing, but I still feel cold. That must be why we never
arrive on time, with our bag full of giblets, those leaky sacks. I'd rather
do that with you and this ache of want and sorrow. I just wish it didn't
hurt more. The brass ring through the bull's nose leads it to clover
or the slaughterhouse, while the tourists and their fanny packs crowd
into churches, dropping loose change into a slot that makes the bells ring.
I'll sing for my supper too, but I need spunky and only a little remorse,
as frogs croak and splash in the pond.

The skateboarders pass in a whoosh, their trucks a lovely wobble.
We work the circuitry beneath the lake as the planets smile benignly
with their dumb, round faces. You saw one rise above the horizon line.
I thought it was a star, but who knows what happens behind those hills?
I'm not even sure what's going on in my own head. It's full of spatters
and loose jelly with someone breaking in when all I wanted was to be free
and maybe a little peace. Turn the lights down and the music up.
This flight is leaving soon.

IT IS ALWAYS DARKEST RIGHT BEFORE THE DAWN

Migrating birds fly from park to cemetery
while keeping a river under their wings.
Someone tried to make us cry until
we stuck those feelings in the freezer
and its still life with shovel and coffin.
Yet tomorrow is a brand-new day, or so
they say, and squirrels just want to have fun
while hurdling the vacuum cleaner.

We should have stayed on the move.
Now my farm is all metal utensils,
but words never fill the spaces.
The bandits have long since been unleashed.
My head hurts from all the pain
and a sports reporter in this locker room
of the soul asking over and over,
Who's trying to take away the future?

The crows are noisier than we are,
and the trucks are louder than the crows,
while we try to rhyme with Coupe de Ville,
depending on how you pronounce it.
Mine is missing its antenna and a hubcap
after getting a rough wash in the quick drip
of our days, lately turning to snow.
Millions of cattle fatten up in muddy feed lots.
We should go on strike everywhere.

There's a crack in the glass, a fire
in the forest, another body outlined in chalk.
One day maybe you'll come back,
just as every time we drive away
the dog watches us from the front window.
Our spaces are a checkerboard of surveillance.
How strange it all sometimes seems,
and why are the men half crazy?

I count the clouds before they disappear,
except even the numbers won't stick.
The fraying starts around the edges,
yet eventually reaches a seam.
Is that what happened to our hearts?
Press REFRESH. Then press it again.
In the deepest silence we disappear,
but it's not here in my earbuds.

PEOPLE, PLACES, AND THINGS

We drive around a lot in cars.
You climbed a mountain without
leaving your room, but I know that
nature is out to get me.
Please create a new username:
mine is yachtsandburgers.
Anything to relieve the stress,
as one life says goodbye to another
before stepping on the ferry
or the chainsaw bites into a tree,
moving on to the next one.
Sound is also static, crunching down
on each word or else it's children
playing in the background.

We got up early to go to the funeral,
missing work and school.
But there's no silence quite like
the snow, so put away the little flags—
the only thing they make are heaps
of you and me. Believe me,
I wish it could be easier,
and a routine physical won't fix it.
Neither will a prescription,
although it might help,
like the signal that tells a flower
when it's time to bloom.
I'm getting closer to the end of this.
Another storm blowing through.

The mule is drawn to the bird feeder,
even though we left it empty.
My corpse sings from the top
of an evergreen, then drags

the trash to the curb.
I don't call it one-stop-shopping,
because it will eventually cost me,
dropping a needle in the cold vein
and skipping Dudley Do-Right.
The music keeps me company,
although I wish it was a phone book.
Whatever happened to that band?
An ambulance idles in the dark.
Here we go again.

FIGHT OR FLIGHT

Spills make the steps slippery in front of the Dollar Tree
where we buy pear-scented shampoo and mayonnaise,
then post #goals to Twitter, because I'm a total bargain
while listening to the air traffic controller tell jokes all day.
Yet every loss wants company like the ghost riders
ready to burn beneath metal palm trees hot to the touch
from a noon sun baking adobe and bones. That weeping
is called history, a ship with black sails and slaughter
now preparing to depart for other worlds until even the stars
are contaminated with us, already are.

Incoming is our mantra, even if it's by subtle degrees,
watching muddy paws and the brutality of a system
chewing through entire species. We traveled so far
from home that it didn't exist anymore, though you
still make the bed each morning, brushing last night's
cookie crumbs onto the floor while asking, *Why do I feel
so alone on the bayou?* There are gardens we can't see.
We listen for the transmission although sometimes
it's only static or a lip bruised on a gravy ladle used
for digging tomorrow's grave.

I never heard the police cruiser coming, with its perpetual
bad hair day, its guns blazing. First the weather report,
then the traffic report, but always the crinkly rustle
of plastic bags caught in the trees like nests for whatever
comes after the human and its stomach pump. After us.
Gunboats secure the tea although now they're drones
cruising silently over the landscape like a hawk
that I read about or saw in HD while a soothing voiceover
narrates the tale of the field mouse gingerly hopping
through patchy ice and snow.

We carved our initials under an iron bridge after driving
our car into a ditch with its row of little turtles.
It made for a good Instagram photo, because Facebook
is depressing. No one likes pickles more than my dad
in a tank top, but I'll stick to thermals tight around
the ankles next to my halo. There's really so much more
to say beyond the nibble, especially when you're starting
at the edge of a cracker while someone knocks at the door
with a branding iron and pink wig talking about the children
and their gods.

On the day of a great jubilee, all debts will be erased.
In the meantime, I activated my credit card after trading
a toothbrush for lunch money and a gesundheit tickling
my throat with a broom. The circumstances of our lives
are just short of crushed, like the one I use to have
on you. No more tangled wishes. No more dirty collars.
Dinner was a comedy of errors scraped into the sink,
and you were mistaken to name it meatloaf. Today the hole
got covered instead of filled, but that's not fixing it
or the noises it makes at night when the music ceases.

ORGAN DONOR

NO CHILD LEFT BEHIND

A satellite flees its orbit
to hide behind the moon,
bending its messages
around a more obscure tidal pool.

There's a rip buried in the fabric.
Friday means pizza for lunch at school.
Some nights we sleep on the roof.
Insomnia also agitates during naps.

We haven't seen a tree for days
as the clouds fold over us
and the carburetor starts to stutter
with soot combed from these wishes.

A knife slices through the center,
spilling sprinkles all over.
We'll move before you tell us not to,
taking the quinine and newsreels.

It's the equivalent of waking up
in a ditch beside the highway,
big trucks rumbling overhead.
But I still won't miss the view.

THE CRASS MENAGERIE

I dream of summer, but it's over there.
I watch a field of throats in bloom.

Shortly after, I came down with the swine flu,
like when the plastic lawn chairs left stripes
the width of bacon on the back of our thighs.
I'd rather take drugs than go out into space,
yet I'll never part with my collection
of pioneering cosmonaut trading cards.
History will try to deceive before it destroys,
but remember, light is matter too.
I find that rhyme makes the edges slightly softer,
because this is a shard of nothing larger,
and nights are sleepless without the boogie.

There's the ghost of a girl in this room.
Some days the rivers run with wine,
other times with flushed pharmaceuticals.
For proper I use a tailor; poetry is the ragged seams.
So why should I feel better at the movies?
Falling out of love is putting your head
through taut harp strings as the loudest trucks rattle
your molars and a character from *Fat Albert*
replaces all the letter v's with b's.
Fireboats bob near the burning platform
while divers plug the leak.
None of them look like nurses to me.
Besides, I only saw the blur of flapping wings.

DARK WATERS

The only thing that fits around our waist is also known
       as a mugging.
It would be redundant to call the police.
The holiday decorations droop beneath the weight
       of their chipper histories.
Half of them will end up curbside with last year's trash;

the rest go in a box stored in the back of a closet
    along with the black bows we wear as hair bands
    or chokers.
Is that why this beginning feels so much like an ending?
Or maybe I stayed up too late again trying to figure out an abacus
    counting hard candies, rent checks, yellow knee pads,
    and your name printed in Braille.
Besides, certain activities are more fun in the dark,
    like denting the appliances with other appliances.
But it's so much bigger than me, each cloud
    with its own trademark.
Sometimes you pass quietly, rubbing into the fur
    of an animal or the officer's collar.
It doesn't have to involve an earthquake or fire.
Blue flecks in the Styrofoam cooler look invisible
    against the lake.
Small candles reflect off the burnished bar.
Later, we watched the river from your window,
    letting something more obscure cast the tiebreaking vote
    between right intentions and cinnamon bun hijinks,
because it's all about the slow drizzle
    and not how quickly you can sear the meat.
Save that for when we're starving cannibals again.
Save it for a trip to Reno.
I never saw the movie version; I didn't even read the book.
The shopping carts are wider than a car
    and fizz like soda when crushed by the compacter.
A sluggish disco ball throws its broken reflections around the room.
No wonder I couldn't find the hook, only a moonbeam.
This might be a good time for a group hug,
    except everybody's on vacation.
Anyway, aromatherapy is a loose category around here.
So too is sand in the steel girders, sunk before the bridge
    was ever built.

SPEED DATING FOR DESIRING MACHINES

The dishes rattle off the shelves
from military flyovers, earthquakes,
subwoofers, and yelling,
    each of them flash-frozen at the peak of ripeness
and shipped cross-country with an oil spill.
As luck would have it,
I was home that day to receive them
    after standing at the window for hours
watching the birds in the yard
do the junky nod-off.
I'm trying to tell this as a story,
just as at a certain point I stopped
    asking you not to go.
So who's now listening to this poem?
Some people get treated like the help;
but when the polar icecaps melt,
we'll all be wearing hip waders to bed
    or else sip a warm beer on a blanket
in the sun and get sleepy.
I might not be able to name 95%
of the plant species I see, yet I know
the unmistakable scent of garlic bread cologne
    worn to speed dating for desiring machines
driving customized bakery trucks stuffed
with Dolly Madison.
That's one way to lose your teeth
after tinkling the ivories.
I mean, love should be the last thing
that takes practice, but it does.
    Sometimes it fucks you up.
But sometimes all the hurt
makes the heart more pure.
And then that heart sprouts ears that hear
    the good frequencies speaking.

Google is our history now,
because I'm done competing with the Mr. Magoo
    documentary voiceover.
I'd rather be a commercial for crash helmets
and satellite trackers.
Every stone has a name.
The nub of the plum is in the white blossom.
The brass birdcage decorates
    a beach volleyball game featuring co-eds
wearing makeshift ankle weights
created from old tires and salt licks
    that the deer now miss.
At twilight,
a couple graze quietly at the meadow's edge.

THE CROWD OF UNKNOWING

Everything went green in the stillness
before the air conditioning kicked in
rattling the sparrows' nest like Magic Fingers
on a cheap hotel room bed,
crooked lampshade where I bumped it
with my knee. That was after
we swerved into traffic and ate dinner
from a plastic take-out container,
barbecue sauce dripping on my shirt
and lipstick smeared across my teeth.

It hurt until Percocet. I took a number
and stood in line at the butcher,
but the only meat left is on my ribs.
There are more powerful forces than me
or even Hogwarts, and I need
to reach the pasture before sundown

where the words are dirty in the grass.
There's so much hate in this world.
In the land of the giants, merry-go-rounds
roll around on their sides.

I've got a turntable in my car that I play
whenever I'm approaching a speed bump,
and this poem is the result. Go ahead
and give it your all; I'm aiming for
about 20% until you give us
our money back. When I got up to go
to the bathroom, someone took
my seat, but that's okay because
I was getting ready to leave,
a paper airplane for my dreams.

The cheese comes straight from the can,
but this just means that like me
it stays fresher longer, except today
when I could barely get out of bed
despite the trash truck idling
beneath my window while someone tries
to stick a refrigerator in it.
There's no hope in that—just the sound
of grinding metal and medical waste
drifting in with the tide overnight.

BLISTER PACK

I never got to say good-bye to the ones who vanished,
only to return wearing gardening masks.
The reception's better in the night sky, anyway.
At least that's how it seemed during long-distance drives
while conducting imaginary conversations with my friends.

Then my life got buried by the present,
which might make this an epitaph,
since every day's an anniversary of something,
though you still can't squeeze it through a tube.

You spent the afternoon chasing a small patch
of sunlight slowly moving across the floor
after today's in-house specials became tomorrow's leftovers.
Some families are ghosts during the holidays.
Lions might gather near the watering hole because they're lazy,
or they may be interior decorators with a mean streak
and a secret hatred for the drama
that doesn't free them from their ribs.

I'm having trouble holding down this piece of paper,
so I slip it under my seat at the movies
where the obvious can be the most difficult to see.
It may have been an unraveling, but I was too busy
taking the park ranger qualifying exam to notice,
and I don't even have a backyard—
just a couple treasured houseplants shaded by a moving van.
Kids are about to get out of school, and it reminds me of cereal,
yet I don't always know what I remember.

WHATEVER FALLS ON THE TRACKS IS NOT AS VALUABLE AS YOU ARE

Brand loyalty is the Alamo. My inner ear is dizzy
where you touch it, like a plastic bag wrapped
around a tree branch. What are the rooms of silence?
They taste of duck as a fattier fowl.
The aftershocks turned the rubble into rubble
and forced people to take shelter on the roads.
But every lintel is a little tilted,

and the forests burn outside our knowing
at least until they reach the stockyards.

If I peer over your head I see a row of billboards
and the pickpocket club planning its family reunion.
The condolence card's color scheme is easy on the eyes,
and also matches the waiting room décor,
as most money is made on the merchandise
after associating with known pornographers
and drug users selling their own form of hope,
because I can only sweat out my addiction to you
with a racing heart in the middle of the night
and a snowfall in the morning.

Now where's that Ativan? It almost rhymes
with abandonment. Yes, those are my footprints
on your pedestal that yells fire in an empty theater
until the house turns against you
while I dream of wrecking the stage with a backhoe.
Still, I'll miss you, and I'll miss you too,
as rows of broken fruit jars get their sticky on,
waved through like a bull to a matador,
like a raccoon on the loose to the cat's spilled food bowl.

The train conductor's job is mostly automated now,
except for the moaning when it's time to go.
I didn't get that message, just the old report card
you left on the kitchen table with a squirt bottle
of stain remover and a chimp named General.
Together they equal out-in-space with the pod doors
closing. Together we didn't equal as much
as we could, except for that summer under
the garden's willow.

ALMOST WORKING

Here we go again   and yet nothing stays
the same   except the usual complaints
about dander on a cat-hair sandwich.
We press plastic leaves in a book to mark
the casualties of wars and fathers   recorded
far from home   in the flash photography
of blinding sunlight.

That's how I learned to be happiest when
alone   watching the clouds dry on
a clothesline   pinned with cutting boards
and their stains.   Motion detectors sway
in the breeze   as if they're being tickled.
My little family likes the taste of vowels.

The inclusive will never be inclusive
enough.   Sharks trail a minivan running
low on gas and provisions.   The police
won't be of much use here   as gravity
eventually gets its way   leaving behind
mouse droppings and the sequins shed
when friends go electric.

Though I've never seen a tornado
in person   we can reenact the damage
wearing raincoats over our aprons
and sipping a Coke.   Some boys wander
by mistake.   Certain predators only hunt
at night   finding an extra set of extremities
near the back of the forest.

FAULTY LOGIC

I'm from the rare generation that didn't go to war,
    but it's still the inheritance.
Air raid sirens wail throughout the mall.
I think about you less on sunny days,
    though I'm just as full of the clichés
    we start with instead of an empty page.
But if this shelter collapses,
    we'll move on to another one
    with free coffee and donuts for the meetings,
    wondering how does it feel to wake up
    in the house in which you'll die?

I'm driven by a machine called protein.
I'm driven by a machine called hope,
    even if at times it's like I'm talking to somebody
    who isn't really there.
The dog might seem aggressive,
    but it mostly wants to play.
So go ahead and rock that boat
    lodged firmly on the shore.
You can call it peace if you want to.
I'll stay here and build it broken
    with the saying instead of the said.

MORNING BREATH

We gather bones for sticks to build a lighthouse or dinghy.
    The best word to rhyme with this is Wikipedia. Dust also falls
upward, just as my cooking show makes the most out of empty cans.
    It's filmed in a room with no windows. Outside, animals migrate

faster than we do except for bears that the circus handlers trained to ride
    a bike in a blizzard produced by snow machines synchronized
with Veteran's Day. There are lots of ways to tumble, not all of which
    involve landing on one's knees, nose to the linoleum.

I don't know where the blankets went while we were sleeping.
    I only live here. Win first, don't last; win last, don't care,
you said before going missing or setting out bowls of trail mix
    at the mausoleum, because there are still moments when I want
to be wiped away like nothing is my own, collecting discarded
    lottery tickets for a destitute gumshoe. All that light gets so heavy;
we could never carry it. Red ivy leaves unfurl across a trellis.
    It must be time for a new paring knife and tin of breath mints.

The paparazzi mistakenly turned me into a celebrity for a day.
    It's not a distraction when the chorus goes out of tune.
A puzzle exceeds its pieces, even a pile of rocks used to keep dogs away
    from the body. The crowd fidgets during the platform-diving
competition judged by Special Forces demonstrating lethal takedown moves
    on the cue cards. If it's not too expensive, I'll try the fish
with the aching gills. Lots of people breathe underwater when an aqualung
    won't suffice or a campfire blows out in a hurricane.

Where are my matches? Stuck to a melted Tootsie Roll in my back pocket.
    I believe in the future every day; otherwise, I wouldn't be doing this,
even if I'm not entirely certain what this is, no matter what the recipe says.
    Studies show that people dream the way they watched TV
as children. A nest stayed intact on the windowsill through the winter.
    My shopping habits are being monitored this very instant while you
scrape the fillings in a spare set of teeth with a steel comb I inherited
    from my father, or do yoga. Whichever you prefer.

It seems to rain every time we go to that restaurant. Maybe that's because
    we always eat the same thing: something that died and something fried.
Plus caffeine. Lots of caffeine to push the raft off from shore, as the boatman's
    steering pole struggles in the mingling of sand and mud, of sex

and puddles of cheap cologne, of ambition and art with a little "a" beneath
    a sky soggy and green, not friends in high places. Now we play
movies on a laptop propped up on pillows, the rug piled with pennies,
    Halloween-costume packaging, newspapers, and dolls.

The self is wispy. What's a commodity and what's debris? We skim off
    a thin layer of salt left on our skin before us and them, as some people
win without a vote being taken. A peanut butter and jelly sandwich
    without peanut butter and jelly is just two slices of bread when history
isn't contagious. It's morning in parts of America, which is more than
    it was before. Talk-show phone lines are jammed with callers asking
what birds use for an adhesive. There's also memory. Who has time
    to put a book together when the pages are still being written?

—November 2008

SPIDER WALK

The tighter the knot,
        the less the light gets through,
unlike that loopy conversation
        we had at the bar,
because sometimes
        silence makes stupid,
as if we could isolate
        the carbohydrates in a cake
while playing fetch
        from the kitchen to the bedroom.

The pictures from my trip
        are still in the camera,
but not everyone believes
        in perception where the spokes
instead of the wheel

          are refracted in shallow water,
because if a toilet runs all night
          and no one's home to hear it,
does it make any noise?

Yet that doesn't mean
          I don't see the cut marks
on your arm,
          which may be why
I only want you to tell me
          about the present and the future,
while the past is a job
          at the wig factory hiding holes
in the top of the head.

CROSSTALK

1)
We don't ask for anything because we like to travel light
or pretend to enjoy Shakespeare in the Park but in reality feel
the animal hurt. You could act it out in a game of charades
with more than a hint of rage or else try to sit quietly with it.
Today we only know what's broken, not including the slivers
of cheddar stuck to the grater or the way we disentangle our ribs
on the drive back to the city, the star map resting small in the palm
of your hand before sliding around a vinyl dashboard
along with loose change for the tollbooth and used Kleenex.

2)
When I'm at peace like this I sometimes suspect there's a tumor
clouding the pain and thoughts set on repeat such as this
whole culture floats on booze and pharmaceuticals,
which is why I'm better off ignoring the phone calls from my bank

along with athletic sex except while wearing an eye patch.
We're born from sand before flesh, and touch soft petals to remember
a face slowly withdrawing into slumber like an orchard's lone
paper lantern buzzed by moths with wings threatened by kerosene.
Every poem eventually gets away from me, and this one has too.
A few of its lines were spoken in a treehouse where you kissed those boys.

3)
It's hard to shut off all the electronic devices, the tuning forks disguised
as egg beaters clanking against the dented insides of a metal bowl
you wore on your head for Easter or was it R2-D2's birthday?
And what about the sped-up metronome with a thing for meth?
I sit in countless official meetings without a clue about Robert's Rules.
You can't imagine what erosion did to Mount Rushmore during
hundreds of thousands of years after we watched a grasshopper land
on the general's ear during a Senate hearing as the sound technicians
licked their lips back in the booth.

4)
I'd describe it as a mall that happens to have runways. It's also
known as death from above, the unmistakable whistle in the day
and the dark. That's when I switched to a hairstylist who only cuts
with a straight razor leaving the edges jagged while she and I chat
about divorce and children. Anywhere can be a VIP section with a piece
of rope and bottles rolling around on the floor, but that doesn't mean
I'm always at your service. Besides, this poem is the equivalent
of a chalkboard on the sidewalk outside a bar advertising drink specials
for the night. This poem's other title is "The Happy Hour."

5)
I'm not so sure that cloud formation looks like Snoopy; to me
it resembles a beetle. I know that tomorrow we'll wake up and things
will be a little better. Yet sleep's no place to sequester hope,
so in the meantime I'll change the sheets while you concoct a smoothie
with whatever's left in the fridge or get creative with mayonnaise,
because turning on the oven seems ridiculous during weather so hot

you fanned yourself with your food while sailboats slowly list
around the harbor all afternoon as if reenacting the battle between
I-don't-care and I-don't-care-more we waged over a dirty rug addiction.

6)
Despite all that, I'm burning brightly right now. We sing along with
downloaded songs played on crappy speakers. The evacuation helicopters
spiral into the sea the way my head eventually came to rest by your side
beneath a loping metal ceiling fan, sunlight seeping through my pores
and an artery throbbing in the right shoulder. Being with you is episodic,
which may be why I've become such a Chatty Cathy with a fondness
for cursing. Or maybe you liked me better when I was slightly desperate
at the electric daisy carnival where you can buy fist-sized lollipops.
Or maybe not. I don't know. I just got here.

ALL THIS DEBRIS IS STARTING TO CLOG THE SYSTEM

the way diesel exhaust
    clings to leaves
and drunks in the bleachers
    throw D batteries
    onto the field.
Meanwhile, we get zapped
    by lasers for lack
    of altitude on days
I miss you
    so bad the soles
    of my feet hurt.
I love the hobbled
    and the speed racers too.
In between
    is the feedlot's maze where
    real estate gets sold

amid miles of unspooled
    garden hoses siphoning
    gas from the refinery
to thirsty bulldozers,
to a row of encroaching
    storm clouds forming
    heaven's breadline.
It's timber time
    across the valley
right when the trees
    are in bloom—
good for combing bee hair;
bad for asthma
    or getting heatstroke
    while wearing a bunny suit.
We flush the kidneys
    clean of their sugar,
then lie and describe it
    as a dry sneeze
    for the camera in authority's
    broadcast booth.

ORDERING OFF THE MENU

All this talk about home   isn't getting us any closer,
      like the thread of you
      I'm always weaving
    while playing chase with the vowels
                      of what goes away.
Maybe that's why I collect shiny things like a crow
and specialize in breath-spray acrobatics
      on a filthy mezzanine nicknamed   The Big Sniffer.
Yet even our careful attentions won't keep the meat

    from sticking to the grill
or answer the questions a soldier asks
    before pulling the trigger.
Butterflies turn black with oil   drifting through currents
    that build a nest in our bloodstream sucking
                                on a synthetic yummy.
I don't have a magazine rack in my bathroom,
    just a framed picture of you
                            dressed up as a Dreamsicle
      for yesterday's escape.
You are what you eat runs the cliché,
and if cranberries flourish in the front yard,
      then it might be a bog.
I get head static,
            both thumbs pushing down   on the ignition
    while water slowly fills up the legroom
of too many commands overwhelming the server we learned
      to play on the piano   with little fingers.
Love flows back if you give it a chance.
      That snag is called   the past.
Someone held up a bank
                  with a bouquet of flowers.
A dented brass band licks the taste   of sweet jealousy
    off a mouthpiece that keeps us reaching for
the wet wipes
        we just got a crush on.

CLEANING UP THE TOXIC ASSETS

    Drag racers lose their traction once
    they hit the glaciers,
    skidding over whatever it is
    that fell out of my mouth.

No wonder we get so hungry sometimes,
chewing on the next person's
seat cushion right down
to the foam and springs
with an animatronic spoiler alert
for an art of war decided
by who blinks first.
A staring contest,
in other words,
where the moistest eyes win.
Sharks surface according to
a separate logic,
though I still didn't know where
I was when I woke up.

The backdrop is a starch and housepaint
dumpling vista where
we frequently lose the signal
having dropped anchor
in familiar shallows rusting Dresden's
scorched orphanages. Vietnam.
The rumblings take place
behind my head,
but that doesn't mean
I hear voices,
just conversations about
the ruined and the new—
you, or the *Little House on the Prairie*
dinner bell before
the invention of plastic cups
and after barbed wire substituted
for the convenience
of a king in the dictionary,
a riveting page-turner
detailing our complicities.

This poem goes faster without
its precious moments—
the seagulls attacking a picnic basket
filled with paving stones
and loose sand,
the forgotten corner of the petting zoo.
This poem steers me.
The crocuses quickly pass
out of season
as we wait at a bus stop
cracking the code
of our longing,
the circuitous route pausing
at every treehouse and
fluorescent-light fixture attached
to a seismograph dropping
a needle to the groove.
If you look closely,
it might appear as dancing,
faces set to the breeze and sun,
the front door pulled closed
behind us.

THE WIDOW'S CLAIM

My pneumonia smells like apricots.
The dropped ceiling makes our hair flat
    but also keeps our teeth from chattering.
I'll fill a notebook with loops to find the language
    of rain brought inside on my shoes.
The only thing to do is push through it.

We're still scavengers, even in our finest clothes,
    reusing travel-size dental floss wrapped around

    a tangle of power cords stored in burial canoes.
I'm like a dirty person with OCD;
you're like a shell game with a small
    rubber ball beneath each nut.

The books feel heavy when they're not being read,
    sliding off the hood of a car.
Some want bombs to take away the pain.
It's only one life among many—
    even an animal realizes that.
So leave a chair out for the extra guest.

The cable guy will give us access to everything
    we've been missing, such as how to knit
    new curtains using orphaned socks.
Improvisation frequently occurs
    within a structure, which isn't the same
    as putting the whole mall on lockdown.

The steakhouse added the tables to its menu,
    just as on warm summer nights I hear frogs
    though not what eats them.
I'm writing this a couple hours earlier.
There aren't any bones in the trash—
    that's not where they get kept.

A WINTER LIGHT FEEDS JUST THE SAME

We only sand down the rough edges we touch
with our hands, while the spy satellites
get distracted by multiple celebrity sightings.
The company that produces them was bought
by another company specializing in artificial
palm trees for corporate lobbies located

right inside the school. Please sign me up
for the weaving class held each night when
the news comes on.

Sometimes it seems as if the whole system
is set to stun, before or after the frightened
livestock gets hoisted by its hind legs—
it doesn't really matter. I mean, who cares
that the coaxing is now slightly nicer? I can't
even squeeze through the chute while wearing
inflatable earmuffs and chaps. In fact,
I'm more in danger of floating off into space,
a small hand learning to let go of the string.

We knew it had snowed without opening
the curtains. You spent the rest of the afternoon
in bed, dozing to the rhythm of plastic
ice scrapers cracking against windshields
in crystal patterns resembling petrochemical
field marshals surveying the battlefield
of freezer-aisle convenience, kinda like how
the Jetsons make food, but not quite.
Then you find yourself weeping for no reason.

A winter light slowly seeps across America.
A winter light blanches a million plasma TVs
and bonus free handheld scanners, as we bury
our fists in jumbo buckets of popcorn
at the movies or disguise Band-Aids
in chocolates before pin-and-mounting
the faded butterfly wings while a dog
strains at its own leash and collar jingling
with trinkets.

I knew your pain for years until the sound
from the intercom became indecipherable.
This is the point where a cartoon parrot
breakdances for cheap laughs. After abandoning
the race along Cookie Road we walked
the rest of the way watching the stars shine
through our dimpled bike helmets, our
inability to stop a slow leak under the sink.
But we had bigger aspirations than that,
along with the darkness to contend with.

We push up daisies every day and grease
our scrapbooks with sticks of warm butter.
In any case, I could never afford that house,
the one where we discovered nails jutting up
from the floor after we took off our shoes and
got intimate with the carpet. The bailout
was slow in arriving as gunmen rushed
through the kitchen, bullets landing in
the soup, apron pockets, and knife drawer.

FAMILY RESEMBLANCES

1)
Today we communicate with everyone in the sky;
yesterday it was with the dead and buried.
We knock dirt from our sneakers
and line up for ice cream after school,
but the dairy will not be literal.
Heads gently wobble on the top of their spines,
like small suns burning over backyards
worn bare by the dogs' anxious pacing,
even though the pack still joins them.

2)
Soldiers sleep under tanks for protection
or to escape the blowing sand.
What's the shelf life for our obsessions?
Please don't cause a big fuss over my holiday sweater—
you know, the one that rolls up over my neck.
The edge of the next diving board will snap off,
making a hat with the fiberglass splinters.
It's happening again, I said to the pines;
but they don't whisper back.

3)
We exited the bank with cash bags empty
and minus our confiscated stick-up note,
rendering the getaway car obsolete.
I don't mind the long walk home alone.
That's why it's called acting.
They want me to write something pretty,
but my lighter got lost under the bed next to
an overused codeine spoon.

4)
Each tongue rhymes with something.
I was happy just to make it across town
dressed as a shark for the chum festival.
Migrating geese fly in a wobbly V, and their victory
is that they don't have to be here anymore.
All the photos turned out slightly blurry.
If I were a taxidermist, I'd stuff it with too much.
Some people love by feeding.

HAPPY CUL-DE-SAC

A honeybee alert makes the same sound
as the stinger. Skull waitresses help me
work out the kinks. Sheets of wax paper
wrap pastries and the butcher's rough trade
in meat that we gather by the armful
for the brief jaunt back to the car
because the domestic will try to train you,
while this poem wants to be free,
hands loosely gripping the wheel.
But don't call me Little Miss Sad A Lot
gumming the candied yams in a happy
cul-de-sac nestled between prescriptions
and the police. In fact, how about
if you don't call me at all?

The sandpaper makes a million tiny stutters
when rubbed against the grain.
If something can't be fixed, then maybe
it's not really broken. I've never dived deep
into the sea, especially after some joker
replaced the lifeguard with a blow-up doll
we watch float over the horizon
where the cruise ships line up to scatter
their trash across the gently curling waves.
A search-and-rescue helicopter circled back
around for another attempt at alleviating
the burden of clouds worn as lightly
as Ian Ziering's sunglasses, as substantially
as mayonnaise sandwiches handed out
by the crew.

Reporting for duty, sir. Otherwise known
as doused with chemicals. Sophie fed a duck
named AFLAC straight from her hand.

If my ribs weren't striated they'd be a carapace.
Even the silhouettes of hawks make the terns
nervous, like scratched-off lottery tickets
that stick with jellyfish to our shins.
In other words, I can only know what
you tell me, as I try to keep it simple
while what's left of my family is out of town.
The glare on the clock face makes it
difficult to discern the time stripping wax
from the finish, except for the stardust
we harbor within us.

A light rain falls on tent cities popping up
in public parks. Some violence is direct
and abrupt, some is slow and subtle.
That makes love the most difficult lesson
with instincts aimed at starvation and feast,
at red leaves or a cold floor. The warrants
are outstanding after we stopped talking
about the past, including the blackouts
and air freshener jingles scrubbing at the sky.
There's one right outside my window,
though it's not the same as what's over you,
just as an electric fence around the garden
doesn't keep out what burrows beneath;
neither does the headdress you wear to the bar.
But my snowshoes are perfect for this
small piece of history we truss up
with rubber bands and poultry string.

COMMON ECONOMIC INDICATORS

The rotisseries may appear to have a chicken sinecure,
but Americans are eating out less these days.

Short a party dress and clapping on cue,
we keep one hand on the wheel, since inspiration
will only get you so far. Just ask the cat—
after lots of licking, he's still going strong.
Technology always shapes the form,
and the windows of opportunity have their own windows.
I guess I should be grateful there's a printout
that I'll be futilely waving in the face of the judge later.

You scrape away the paint as soon as it dries, making
portraits from the flakes, from the roots buried with a star
silhouetted by a searchlight briefly sweeping away the sky.
Why do we tell stories more often at night?
Who's keeping track of Iraqis killed by the war?
From here the view is next to torn.
Fans constantly cool the servers and their information
is consumption by another name I forget in the feeding.
Or big and sticky and I can't get it off me.

Collision is a combination of both speed and mass.
Squirrels are adroit at getting to the birdseed.
It can be precarious to sit alone in a room
watching exhaust spill over a horizon line blue
as the pills made by pharmaceuticals.
Sometimes it makes sense to nibble around the edges,
other times to swallow the whole piece.
We hide mirrors under the floorboards to honor the mines
dug with fireflies clinging to sharp pant-leg creases.

Melt everything down so it fits in a fanny pack,
starting with the best behaved and then switching to sunspots,
because returning can be harder than going away.
Blood vessels constrict in an air-conditioned foyer
med-school interns know as big-box-store syndrome.
An electronic press release denied the presence of asbestos
lining a covered bridge that hides the horses' mistakes,

their bulging eyes of clotted milk blurring the calendar leaves
and daily specials written on a dry-erase board.

We found them during a game of paranoid word search
during which we negotiate the fees for living,
asking, Where exactly does outer space begin?
Right above the dollar-store awning and a Buick's leather seats,
the plastic-bag sculpture threaded through a chain-link fence,
the old mattress used as a trampoline.
My handwriting in high school was rounder than it is now,
but amateur psychic spoon-benders still admire the curve
of a willow hiding a swing in its long branches.

Pardon the interruption, but this is where I feel most free.
Lawn chairs take the legs out from under hunting;
besides, I had enough trouble just getting up for work.
You made it as far as a blown fuse and the pork loin aisle
with its slit bellies slid across a glass counter.
There's also thunder without rain
and rush-hour traffic stretching back to the country,
which gave us the chance to change into bathing suits
while pretending to remain relentlessly upbeat,
i.e., as free wine tastings are to the grape.

Saltwater helps keep our small heads bobbing
in the slender translucence between the sand and the sea
near a tailgate party with burst balloon music
that won't make us better or worse for the disappointments.
I'm happy just for the chance to be with you.
The words look different without their bodies.
Condiments hardening in jars rattle whenever
the refrigerator door is tugged open by a local news anchor
taking one imaginary ski lesson at a time.

First you stand up and dust yourself off.
Assembly-line photo albums come with their own set of pictures.

You took others of offshore oilrigs, deviled eggs, beer,
lots of beer, and amateur magic tricks after they happen.
All the adults in Charlie Brown mumble,
as if the astronauts misplaced their teeth,
because sometimes this world isn't ready for home,
armed as we are with glitter glue squeezed from a canteen.
I might as well be writing about candy.

TICKET TO RIDE

We leave a light on at night
and fall silent by the morning
as kelp beds tickle our sleep.
I try to make it right by you.
I try to finish off Caesar.

There's a flesh behind the ghost
and a ghost behind the flesh.
Mail drops through the door slot
during a billing cycle ranging
from Zen to vent.

Miniature ponies weigh more
than me, which I only realized
when I leaned up against one
wearing a tilted party hat.
Together we trot in perky circles.

Then I remember the future,
its dorsal fin in reverse a blue
corona. The language on our hands
is too small to read, so fingerprints
are the jailers' transcription.

But I hope my friends know how
much I love them, because I'm
not treating this as a poem.
Car stereos blossom in the heat.
Salt collects along our hems.

MERCURY IN RETROGRADE

I used to know ghosts   now I know you—
     a thin blade nestled under my ribs.
But I prefer that to the small houses sheltering a fist.
If you ignore it in waking life,
                          it may return in your dreams.
A fight broke out at the bar called Mother's,
     as we watched from across the street.
A squad car pulled onto the sidewalk,
its engine hovering
              in the sky above.

The pine trees look real enough.
An aster is both a flower   and a star.
This is the only letter I can write you
                           at this moment,
     like when you wanted to name the new dog Pepsi.
Desire is the pursuit,
              which means sometimes I can't sleep,
though we still get up for work the next day
     with its metaphors for paperwork
and an employee fridge full
                  of expired food.

The machines hum in the background
     as we carry the clock from room to room.

It'll take longer to get home
                        in these weather conditions
    working their way
        down the page.
The advertisements are faster with tendrils
    tipping tombstones in a yard scrolling
        through hundreds of satellite channels.
Yet there's a quiet outside   after the snow stops
that briefly arrests
            each departure.

It's not called a poem,
                and besides it's already over.
Legless bellboys are all cap.
Butterflies swarm the eyes of cayman,
while we fill a windsock with pistils and mortars
    serving as today's neatly filed flight plan.
I'm unsure about tomorrow.
So how did my vision of karma
                    come to include retribution?
There's always one kid in elementary school
    who ate yellow snow
            even if he didn't.

It's gut-check time for the body without organs
as the usher tears the tickets in two
    despite every seat being taken
amid the tanks painted pink   and a crisp-shirted governor
shoving in line for gumbo
                while giving the sneeze guard a workout.
We learn the spells without effects,
    which I then save to my computer.
My headphones fall off
           whenever there's a tremor.

Not so with diabetes   you have to eat it before it eats you.
Maybe that's why I'm always thirsty
       while you're busy learning to let go.
Update: My drug-dealing ex-neighbor turned his son into a runner.
I don't believe in angels,
               but they occasionally speak to me.
And I'd take the measure of things, as you suggest,
       except the ruler doesn't bend.
Let the crystal in the heart be hard yet translucent.
A wish is only a stutter toward
                   the last days of the war.

SPLIT THE DIFFERENCE

Big seagulls stick close to the trashcans in winter,
except where a chuck wagon washed up on shore.

I usually pay for whatever I eat.
The bus stop offers a little bit of shelter.

I know it's beautiful on the other side of that wall,
but for now we'll keep tracing patterns on the bathroom floor.

It looks like marble, yet it's actually plastic.
Without an online presence, I'm barely there.

The mind makes a humming sound while driving late at night.
It's a law of physics that matter seeks to dip in the middle.

This might explain what happened to our holiday party
with its animated fruit basket wobbling in chiaroscuro.

The age of heretics has passed.
The shadows of bodies fall upward too.

We're already members of the knitting circle.
Later, we'll disperse into the swarm.

It's not my job to guess your motives,
but I still have to wear a tie to work.

Push the pin through right below the neckline
is what the elevator-repair manual says.

Hopefully the higher floors won't go underwater
where the GPS points us to the disappearing trees.

Whatever happens on the couch can be described as willy-nilly.
There are so many flavors of gum to choose from!

If you're still unsure, file under the letter "O";
coincidentally, that's where I last saw my top.

A TRUE STORY   IF YOU BELIEVE IT

The people on land   look tiny from sea,
and vice versa.   Either way time will eat us
alive.   At some point the humanities
will no longer be with us.   I just hope you
can finish your book   before then.
I remember not getting   with the program,
and this poem   might go straight to DVD
after a subtle nod   to the hot air balloon
passenger-basket weavers   and the mall rats
suffering from dehydration   by the foundation.

If poetry has the most to lose   then it could
risk more.   Sophie kept the starfish alive
in a toy bucket cracked   with dreams of escape.

There's also a grace   to surviving,
and rules we follow   without knowing.
Even so   I miss talking with you on the phone
while watching dancers rest   in a meadow
of gym mats   as loose strands of their
hair are woven into nests   for the lonely.
I carry most of it   on my computer.

I once split my head open   on a cash register,
then was paranoid for weeks   about losing
my job.   I told the bus driver, and she said:
Next comes restless   then comes desperate;
better to get off here   at distracted.
The vegetables   grow into October.
After that you can pretend   it's a baked potato
in paperback   and shot full of holes.
I'll admit that I have   certain obsessions.
This year's harvest dance   takes place in the barn.

THE ALCHEMY OF MORNING

The lion stores gold in its mouth and yawns at the sun.
Would it be better if its teeth were tight with braces?
The lost objects come back in different disguises, like a catalog
that specializes in last-minute gifts. This one smells of mint
and wet cardboard boxes tossed with ski poles under the bus.
It's rough terrain even for hang gliders. Imagine how the future
farmers feel. This isn't the United States of America. I sometimes
imagine a strobe light when it's only a faulty bulb. On certain days
everything vibrates slightly and speaks a language of hum.
That doesn't have anything to do with enjoying nature or not,
or whether I'm a regular at the closest bar.

The gears grind whenever they're shifted hard into neutral.
That won't stop the runaway mining cart headed for a large gap
in the tracks. In my dream, it exploded in an exaggerated fireball.
You said, I'm glad it's behind us now. My view of life is incomplete.
There was nothing left to do with the piles of empty beer cans
except resize them as jpegs for the web. I donated my collection
of giraffe neck protectors to the Smithsonian. You can see them
in the modern wing with Wu-Tang Clan memorabilia and an oil
portrait of my father as a hat shop. I meant to say a velvet painting
of Barbara Walters conducting an interview with Yuri Andropov.

Fast food restaurants create a logic for the burger. I shared
a hair color rinse with Lindsay Lohan. That sound is of the other
shoe dropping, except that sometimes you never hear the first one.
Or maybe it's just the click of a dog's nails on the bare floor.
Still, I don't have any pictures of pets on my Facebook page.
When I hear the word bricklayer, I also think of basketball.
Are we taking it really slow or just ignoring each other?
The award for wearing the biggest backpack to the rap show
is called logorrhea. It's fun to imagine the things you can laminate!
It might even take the musty smell out of that wet bath towel.

We keep a telescope inside to find stars on the ceiling
but mostly end up staring at the TV. One screen was even bigger
than my daughter and washed the room in Easter egg colors.
I listen to the radio with the speakers pointed away. The photographs
tell us what we already know. The guardrail has more than
a few dents in it beneath pink magnolia blossoms sagging
in the rain. Yet once the invisible pen dries out, the writing
will be even harder to read. I didn't touch your money. I'm here
to rearrange every solitary corona as the back of the class blurs
for the nearsighted teacher.

PUSH BACK AT IT

Like hummingbirds we get drunk

                on sugary cocktails and bright colors

in Icarus regard for the deceptive

                blue skies of fall.

The tale's spinning can be more interesting

                than the story itself.

Addiction has long claws that wrap around

                and through.

Bees gather freon from our

                neck pendants.

In the meantime, please rescue us

                with a credit card.

Language tells me what

                to do.

I mean, we try to make sense

                of things,

but our sense contains some

                nonsense too.

BREAKING AND ENTERING

It's like being at the office
when you're not around
or else I'm neatly stacking
prosthetics in a closet running
the length of a food trough.
We hand crank the generator
when the electricity starts to flicker
outside the hospital walls.
It's false to imagine the body
immune—just ask the orphans.
I know that place, with its
faux-grainy, dark-wood paneling
and famine on the TV.
Every Friday night
the Clanging Bedpan Band
plays there for free.

The dog looks eager to march
in a parade featuring used
barbecue basting brushes.
Where the refrigerator truck
backs up to the dumpster
we make temporary rooms
with cable box pomade.
Exhaust fills the staircase
like an obese panda bear,
like when we have trouble breathing,
watching life-size spinal-
adjustment dioramas sell
briskly at a science museum
gift shop's after-Christmas sale.

From the warehouse to the White Castle,
from the Ferris wheel to the people mover,
this is a love poem
as smooth as a missing tooth.
Sunlight fades the book's cover.
At least we have some control
over the heat this year,
and won't need to warm
the kitchen with a microwave oven.
Let the red-faced warbler finish singing—
it's been known to attack
spontaneously, swelling retinas.
Curious gardeners teach
the art of tending; we're still
obsessed with endings.

THE CARNIVORE'S DILEMMA

1)
A truck hauling scrap metal
ended up on the heap.
The moral arc may be long,
but its interruptions are constant.
From the ground, the horizon
shrank to a view down
the glistening nose of a bugler
summoning the troops as
the skies above opened up.
No need for a scuba suit now
that it all floats on the surface,
beginning with an apology
and ending with a full shopping cart
in front of Walmart.

At some point I stopped believing
in fate because it wasn't
getting me anywhere.
A new skin forms along
the milk carton's rim.

2)
Small, hard June bugs collect
on the screen door of
a laundromat offering free Wi-Fi.
We ate eggs in the hole
for breakfast, then sweated
them out later while trying
to pitch a tent on the sidewalk
outside the nail salon.
It could be much worse
compared with the mistake we
once made with creamed spinach
fattening us up for slaughter
when I only wanted to cuddle.
Well that changes everything!
We sip beer from a used
Dunkin' Donuts coffee cup
instead of getting a haircut
after another night
of fierce electronics.

DEDICATION

Don't tell me those are chickens when they're really rhinestones,
even if my designer handbag was made by Mildred Wattles.
For a living, I sing in the back of the bar because
nothing puts me on edge quite like Up with People.

Are we rushing toward the train or is it rushing toward us?
In any case, there's a huge thing headed this way.
I don't see any tracks, just a calendar's glossy photo of a lake
and a pair of sneakers left on a small wooden dock.

In other words, time rolled over you, then it rolled over me,
or else we're sitting in an amusement-park catapult that lost its torque
as the teenage attendants busily check their text messages.
Sometimes I don't know where all the words come from.

Yet for now I'm fine with this ball of confusion.
That's why I'll claim a logic in firing randomly at the target.
And I'll never remember the names of everyone in this room,
which kinda makes it resemble online dating.

You're like what the buttercup falls in love with.
Certain versions of dinner theater in the Everglades include
wrestling alligators given regular cortisone shots in the jaw.
Mine were for the inner ear and wrong dumbbell selection.

THE PASTORAL IS INSIDE YOU

Usually it would feel good to be home
on the coldest day of December,
but I can't smell and chew simultaneously,
which I only realized after watching
a furry dog drop its rubber toy in order
to sniff the nearest lamppost
and recalled—mistakenly, it turns out—
a python nearly getting the best
of Marlin Perkins with lots of flopping
around in muddy, shallow water
during the steady voiceover narration.

This was right after we gave the snooze button
a serious workout as the rooftop satellite
TV dishes changed color from gray to silver.
Part of the security training involves
getting tasered. I still don't like categories,
and I'll be moving again soon,
packing everything in a hatbox drawn on
with magic markers and wrapped in
wrinkled cellophane after I forgot
the combination to the padlock
and dropped your last letter in the snow.

The animals helped keep us warm,
right where the collarbone shows.
It's the sense of instincts and their quiet
rhythms of loss, not found on the calendar,
such as I digress but don't defer while
watching the leaves slip into hibernation.
They're somewhere in the middle of that tree
or else blown away with the candy wrappers
and our porn quota while following moths
to the basement's fluorescent bulbs
that flicker and are extinguished.

Giants use haystacks for nests lined with
expired vats of candied yams even the freegans
wouldn't eat after sampling the baker's buns.
The storm that passed through last night
has since moved up the coast,
like trading too many DUIs for a bike
that we're lucky to get out of the driveway
without damaging the decorative hedges.
So you keep the wine and I'll keep the roses,
and remember to be gentle.
People are trying to sleep in the other room.

FUTURE TENSE

It's so late in the antenna fields
    it just might be early, so reach
  through the broken windowpane
and unlock the door.
                      We carry
    one stone to the next, storing
  piles of wet towels and bone bruises
in a yellow birdhouse,
                      because
    all narratives are ultimately elusive,
  speaking to the dead as much as
to the living.

I don't like the cold, but I like
    the seasons, each with its own
  brand of big-league karaoke.
Loss can be comforting,
                      though disappointment
    is another story. We eat
  for no reason. My vintage calendar
collection etched in spent
                      shell casings
    was damaged in a flood started
  while fishing in the bathtub
with flea collars glued to a stick.

The result? A few frozen TV dinners
    and a field that blooms with little
  hands smelling of magic markers.
When I looked up
                      an hour later,
    the sun had already set.
  The least we can do is protect
the children. Then let's have that drink.

This time around,
the rollover involved a dog and a strip
of chewy beef seen from a taxi stuck
in traffic on its way to the airport.

CURIOUS GEORGE GOES TO THE BEACH

The bayou garden's petro sheen
laps a dinner bell where
swallows hide their nest.
The push reel mower
got a second wind once
the Benzedrine kicked in,
leaving a table filled
with rosé and ashtrays for
the wedding party crashers.
I've come to like your lies
turning everything less square,
just as folding a flag that way
makes it resemble a sandwich
packed with crooked salutes
and hard of hearing.
Sometimes a door closes in front
of us, and sometimes behind.
The car alarms in the parking
lot are only a nuisance
and don't deter turtles from slowly
migrating across the blacktop.
The Green Lantern needed
a helicopter to keep up
with the other superheroes,
but we're still arriving late
to *Annie* rehearsals
with a forged doctor's note

written in a prescription-
shopping delirium,
because history is the same
as checking in with the disease.

I never knew this language
to stick to anything except
a mail carrier's can of mace.
It's not always insomnia
that makes it difficult to relax
when the heart feeds on itself.
But I don't have nine lives—
maybe three at most,
and I've already used up two:
the first one went down
with the ship while clinging
to the captain's legs;
the second when you punched
a hole through the drywall.
Or maybe it was a carwash mishap
that simultaneously scrubbed
away the traces.
We filmed it all low budget
until we got distracted
by the flicker around the edge
of things and the stony silence
involved in letting them go.
Besides, any new rumors
can't be as bad as the ones
that already exist.
At least that's how it seems
in the midst of a food fight.
Somewhere in this apartment
are grains of beach sand—
the towels and plastic sunglasses
long since put away.

THE ENVIRONMENTAL MOVEMENT

Not a star, but the part of the star that breaks off
                                            in the dark.
I'm happiest when I travel light
                       and do minimal damage.
Who cares if it flies crooked,
    as long as it's got wings?
Our art flies broken so that we don't have to.

What's advertising but making a desire static?
The last one to look back
                      steps deeper into time,
    with its pile of clowns tottering on a unicycle.
I've got bills to pay;
                 the visions will have to come later.

This is the last day the sun will shine on us this way,
    so let's go get boozy by the pool.
I don't know where the trails of sparks
                            will fall.
On the forests.   On the beds.   On the waters.

DOCKING BAY

COST OF LIVING

We might burn down half the block with these homemade fireworks,
    but the proof, as they say,
         is in the pudding,
    and I'm avoiding dairy.
The power company locked out its workers during a heat wave.

Little juice boxes are what inmates get to drink.
We didn't have another place to stay
                    once the corporation became a person
    who doesn't need a job.
So why am I the one always apologizing,
    as you're sawing off the legs?

Behind the billboards is a desert;
                behind the green is scorched earth.
The real is its own form of fantasy,
    a row of dolls stacked skull to skull.
The celebrity divorce involved a big payment,
                  but my check is in the mail with cinderblocks
    and a side cramp from drinking too much soda.
A plant will twist and reach for the light,
               while we're still clapping to turn on the lamp,
like role players sitting at a table,
hand raised to strike or caress.

An octopus is the surround sound of the marine world,
    yet I'd rather stand in the sun denting cans of sterno,
and if that doesn't work,
             I can always catch a train,
since my apartment is the station,
    along with the grammar police.
Maybe we should set up a lunar base;
                the views would certainly be better than from here
and its fifty blind spots,
           its empty grain silos reached by canoe.
All I know is what was later taken.
All I know is what you give to me.

DUMB LUCK

The same song played on a loop all afternoon,
though that's not what we mean by the low-end workout.
The less sanctioned stuff happens around back
while I bury the evidence of another failed meal
and you break school rules with the boys.
There must be more information somewhere
on the website. Bodies at high velocity collide harder,
except on Saturn where they sing in a chorus.
It's not as if I've been probed by aliens,
but let's say that we've gotten familiar.
You forget that I used to work as a ranch hand
where every beast is immortal. Now I sew
unwashed socks for hoof-and-mouth disease,
because first they bring out the water cannons,
then they just shoot you in the face.
Tell me again what's the color of your purse
and the ingredients in Junior Mints.
You might start the evening with a drink;
I'd rather two-time the pharmacist's pharmacist,
which is easier than saying, Just give me the loot.

We've come so far, and yet we've barely left
the porch. Still, there are children involved,
and monsters to defeat, some of which are inside me.
Luckily, they're susceptible to spells resting
our shrunken heads on a mushroom blooming
everywhere else amid the knife play banned
along with opposable thumbs. Each new era
gets shorter and shorter. Soon they won't
bother to call our names, as every desire
exceeds its object, even in the dark,
and I'm a machine of consequence, such as
Operation Empty Candy Wrappers is in full effect.
Right here, right now. There is no other place

I want to be. Unless we're talking about a medevac.
Or maybe just more meds and a refrain
that goes hurt, hurt, hurt I took on tour with me
to sell t-shirts along with a round of hangman,
because when a hum tickles between the teeth,
a poem is close to being finished.

This one isn't. First we need to let the dog off
the leash and stick the spurs in the horse.
Eventually, the waters will rise to meet us,
but for now it's only warmer in the sun,
your neck arched longer than a riding crop
stirring sediment beneath the berries or swinging
from a chandelier like Bunny Wigglesworth
on kitsch retainer mocking the politicians.
Next comes the waiting stage, which we're
less good at, all bodice-ripping if I wore one—
instead, there's a haunting behind the ribs.
The pit master told me that the meat gets juicier
the longer it sits, but that seems counterintuitive
for those preferring sloppy seconds to the cleanup crew
burnishing ivy on the walls, as if I could give
a fuck about the self-appointed leaders.
I dress myself and sometimes you, picking clothes
up off the floor. Beneath that floor is where
I'll be buried, gravediggers at the ready.
I was one until I strained my elbow returning
crisp backhands. But I've still got a fighter's chance,
even if I'm terrified of needles.

Besides, I only dream about people who go away,
although I'm happy about your cottage by the sea.
The unfurled heads of pink hydrangeas bow
slightly on their stems. Even the slaughterhouses
have been streamlined for efficiency,
like spotting drug addicts by their sweat,

as the hook connects a carcass to the chain.
Yet cognitive therapy is going to kill my poetry,
and a funner version of cheese and crackers
is called cheesecake. We can be bought
for the right price—for instance, here in the city
I haven't seen the stars for weeks, just the glint
of a biochemical pendulum. There's no warehouse
for what perpetually gets loose, such as
a bank robber without a bank, lots of stick 'em up
to no one in particular, except for the flabby streaker
who tired himself out before the commercial break
was over. It's all in a day's work, or at least
an afternoon.

For the rest of us, it's about corralling hornets
with the deckhands and a captain passed out
behind the wheel of a company car customized
with golf ball washers, a rusted deli meat slicer,
hairy Hobbit-feet slippers, and a marketing
campaign bigger than the GDP of some small countries.
No wonder you walk around with a moving box
under your arm, otherwise known as hedging
your bets, forgetting that I've already marked
the cards with an escape plan featuring me
banging my head against the wall, which isn't
a version of winning but rather extending the game.
Groups of soldiers move through the yard on patrol.
I've learned some lessons badly, and, sure,
I've got a few regrets; but was it really so wrong
to root for the Borg against public displays
of affection? I'm going to be twice as dangerous
when I'm part machine. In the meantime,
I'll stick with this wooden splint doubling
as a tongue depressor or a birdhouse in the basement.

DISCONTINUOUS SIGNAL

The arsonist might start out anonymous,
but everyone has a story to share,
even if like me they have trouble
    reading music.
The space invaders travel past protein,
yet are confused by the way
    flip flops fit.
Blue isn't the color of aquariums.
It's what we see in our prisms,
as afternoons thrum like a faint muffler behind
    a nest of voices.
Still, I don't have a horse in this race anymore,
just a sore neck from staring at the gargoyles
    until they turn transparent.
Besides, someone keeps moving the finish line
with a corporate report
    on the animal kingdom.
Let's call it my +1, and then compare enamel
after personally inspecting each traffic sign . . .
    starting now.
A Budweiser truck blocks a ski lift
    at the Olympics.
Instead, we took a junior rollercoaster for those
who feed extra meatballs to the dog
or leave them in a shiny gift box
    under the Christmas tree.
Eventually, the clouds moved in and filled the sky
    with thunder.
This may be the only line I write today,
    and even then it's slurred or crooked.
It's a song so dirty I had to switch to porn
    when my mom walked in.
So tell those space invaders there's a hole
in the windsock where the toes

    are supposed to go.
It's partly how I ended up with a closet
of cheap suits and noise after the managers
took away all my berets
    with sand in their tight headbands.
Everything else is just a reflection.
Silence isn't golden—
    it's closer to gray.

I LOVE A PARADE

The orchards come down in a barrage
of shower caps, setting the fireflies free
to extend their brief lifespans.
That's how I came to be called the Price Chopper,
singing a different kind of tune.
All these letters form a little heap
we're forced to walk around,
but that doesn't mean I invented the dance known as
a drink and the two-step.
In fact, I'm mostly bored with cocktails,
even the ones that come with miniature umbrellas
and flaming tiki heads in a tall glass etched
with an image of the sea.
Still, I've got the makings of a professional.
I'd collect bird nests except we live
in a desert.
The convention hotel is built on a fault line
running the length of a nearby highway.
We stayed so late the chairs were stacked around us
as our dreams got even weirder.
But that's much better than having them taken away
while sending stock images through
the ether with a tracking device

weathered for the elements
like a wrinkled tarp, rubber hose, or kitchen sponge
placed to soak up the river's silted run-off.

Everyone rides the bull these days.
We moved into an apartment complex on the edge of town
that was a favorite of shale field workers.
But the blizzard in October surprised us,
wrapping white grocery bags
around our shoes so that it looked as if
we were standing in the clouds.
I didn't invent that dance either,
at least according to my handwriting analyst
and the despair that occasionally overtakes me
at the sight of the wrecking ball
and everything I tightly clung to now gone.
Or almost gone. Or eventually will be.
No wonder we decided to eat in today,
though that doesn't explain what happened
to those meatballs—
except for the pieces of food stuck
between your teeth.
I'm not going to say it won't occur again,
but I'm guessing it will be different next time,
the talons close to the heart
digging a little less deeply into
the salmon's flesh lifted from the water.
Another channel features cubic zirconia earrings
on sale until the end of the hour,
after which the programming switches back
to local news and a report
on military homecomings.

PRICE OF ADMITTANCE

The diving bell doesn't make a sound,
though the air is filled with leaflets.
One day we'll crack through the enamel.
That's not what's making the refrigerator stink
or keeping the pile of old magazines
from turning into a fire trap; but if science
taught me anything, it's that all matter
is combustible. There's even a little gas station
on Mars. We get coffee and a danish
from the same place every morning, next to
the laundromat that closes early on the weekends.
Sometimes I don't know where else to go.
The funny thing is that I can see your house
from the train. One day I want to live
closer to the river. For now, I'm slowly
developing the memory of an elephant,
if that elephant was completely stoned.
It's better than the Hannibal stomp
or the dusty furniture stored in the basement.
Either way, it's probably going to cost me,
with the ingredients for each McDonald's
franchise delivered by truck. Tracking dopamine
is the least of the neurologist's worries.
It helps to loosen the hairnet. What else
was the coach's son supposed to do?
I'm still waiting to meet my first saint,
while at the bank, machines count the money.
If I was a magician, I'd cast a spell called
honey boo boo; instead, I watch it on TV.
Let me know when you're coming back,
and I'll try to leave a light on.

THE FAST AND THE FURIOUS

The wiggling at the worm farm
slowed down during the blizzard,
but a blackout is different—
it's when the circuitry shuts down,
a ribcage fusing with the refrigerator door
and its array of hardening condiments
that mirrors a bus kneeling at the curb,
because sometimes this is what desire does,
as we make a collage of these histories,
the flags unraveling according
to their patterns taking a tumble down
the insulin tunnel, the free needles
distributed in the candy wrappers.

Better if you just pass me a tissue
that I'll hold up to a wave thickly veined
with saline and clotted with oil,
the sweat crashing beneath the skin
where your hand gently passes,
or I could spice this poem up with
a little sex and violence from the movies,
even though you're all the viva
I could ever need, as the cruise ships
navigate a harbor dredged for their depth,
lifeboats at the ready even this close
to home—or especially—right there
beneath your window.

You can say it's like being healed
and actually mean that the pain
doesn't hurt as much, yet I'm not
making this up as I go, but rather
found myself surrounded by a cold

metallic sheen, everything post-robot
and, Here, take this little blue pill,
evaporating water from the hemoglobin
until the blood browns whereas
the semaphore pinkens—I'm not sure why,
I'm not a scientist, and instead follow
the trade winds while sweeping out
the cargo hold with its rats disappointed
by the Bauhaus.

THE THIRD WAY

I tried to take out a patent on mittens,
    but the Wellbutrin beat me to it.
Instead,
        I became a unicyclist
   seeking to avoid the low clothesline.
On the other side,
                ectoplasm can get kinda messy.
Memory in the harvest fields falls beneath
    a sharpened plow covered in
                        seeds and glitter.

At a certain point,
                we couldn't keep the band going.
Maybe it was all the time we spent responding
    to our boss's emails
                or haggling over the cost
    of popsicle sticks used to make
                      leaky boats.
My tongue swells up with split the difference.
Then we click on every link
    as the pixels grow bigger than the screen.

Tonight's as quiet as pollen drift,
    or at least it was for a minute
                                once the dentist
                finished a round of house calls.
Shark nets protect public beaches.
For years I had no idea what a slider was,
    except for its stretch
                          in my waistband.
No matter,
        the language of love is better in translation.

A LITTLE HAUNTING IS A SWEET PAIN

The sparkle meter twitches whenever you stand near it,
but that's okay because you always want your crush
to be a little trashy. Every message breaks a heart somewhere,
though the animal bodies encircle us with warmth.
Not only the government conducts surveillance,
yet my twig collection briefly confused them, whether
used to build a nest or for kindling. Meanwhile,
I'll wait for you at the bar as the sun sinks into the river
while wearing the railyard like a skirt. In other words,
I couldn't miss you any more than right now, though if I do,
I know it's going to hurt.

Go ahead and lather up the flagpole—it won't take away
the stink. Besides, the headless horseman has the worst orgasms.
Yet at least we're close to the park and its quarry
for throwing the first stone while groping around in a blackout
and chased by a song, because I'm never going to lie,
but I'm going to make a lot of shit up. Just don't
get me started on the country club at Sleepy Hollow.
Helicopters are a form of optical illusion, so show me again

how to land this thing. Clouds stack on the horizon line
like pillows at the top of your bed. Earlier, we stopped
for allergy medicine and a wedge of cheap fudge.

It all started innocently enough on Gchat; when it was over,
we couldn't pay the rent. Yet I've gotten much better
at endings. Perfectly reasonable people have extraterrestrial
experiences, but I'm not one of them. We still live
in the shadow of the castle, with inflatable alligators bobbing
in the moat, although I don't have an alibi for the occasion,
and it should be obvious by now that I'm terrible
at telling stories. Maybe this time you can let me off
with a warning instead of making me bring donuts to the judge
after uploading the video link and snorting diet pills.
No wonder I'm always hungry.

TREES AND THEIR TENDER MAINTENANCE

The future is a wish in reverse
we waited for in the doorway.
There's a silence louder than any explosion
at the movies, louder than your breathing
in the middle of the night.
I'm plugged in for the dropout
with chubby thighs bunching in spandex
during Dick Cheney's exercise routine.
After the patrons leave,
a waitress wipes down the table.
Yet I can't go back and change the past.
The present is a dirty carpet,
a big dirty bird. Cumulus clouds today,
like a god left the cap off the toothpaste or something.

But kids say the darndest things.
We make our gravy from slender packets
the way mom used to do,
though too much salt or sugar hiccups my system,
which isn't the rumor that will sink my campaign.
The arborist keeps track of broken limbs;
squirrels keep track of the arborist.
A blimp gives slow tours of the crop circles,
including the ones etched into our rooftop garden
as well as the local butcher shop,
because all that meat doesn't grow on trees—
it hangs from hooks.
Just don't tell those adorable kittens on YouTube.
One even plays the piano for treats.

MEMORIAL FOR THE MEMORIALS

The celebration of performed mourning comes straight through the TV
with its tanker trucks in low formation buzzing the houseplants drooping
from neglect after we went missing just long enough not to be noticed,
though more by the bosses than by our friends, who sometimes go missing
too; but that's okay since we've pushed our poker chips all in on this economy
of loss, minus one exchanged for a hamburger, fries, and whatever's
left over from the hydroponics convention where the stage is front-lit
so that nervous speakers can't see the crowd or in this case the empty
round tables, water glasses trembling slightly when the elevators jam
as the carry-on poodles trapped inside gulp down precious oxygen after
each sharp bark.

In other words, it might start imperceptibly, then eventually disappear,
leaving not even a shadow in its wake but rather a bone density scan
with the results emailed west of the Mississippi, though not as far as
Sacramento, possibly somewhere in Kansas or maybe Kent State if
relocated by a UFO and its histories of Jupiter preferable to our own

with its how many people killed then, and how many exponentially more
ten years later, snatching the house keys from our hands while passing out
big bonuses before the holidays now occurring each week, as the stores
prep their accompanying sales, including this rack of last year's styles
and the greeting cards that play a tinny tune, such as "Greensleeves,"
"The Star-Spangled Banner," or "Smells Like Teen Spirit," and are also
secretly programmed to yodel.

But you're gonna have to pay extra for that feature, which means adjusting
the foam padding poking through the ripped seams that I'll press tightly
together until my arms give out or else get in line and take a big number,
and for what?—the chance to take another very big number, and maybe
a glimpse of the landfill with the crowds pushing past as the day traders click
refresh, and the lawns mowed by someone else, and signs separating
from their backing, and text messages, and reporters just missing the story,
and children lining up before and again after school, and butter melting
in plastic wrap, and Tumblr, and waves that gently break over our heads,
and clean bedding, and celestial harmonies, and trash pickup in the early
morning, and blood sugar spikes, and omnivores, and more gas in the car,
and the form that doesn't hold.

Even the brightest ashes fade before reaching the ground, following lines
of scaffolding leaning heavily against a building where pigeons warily nest
and you made a bed with three blankets, a radio tuned to the news
as if we could touch the vanished while stars and planets scatter across
a darkening sky, though I still think it's better if you cover the early mornings
and I take the late-night shifts; we'll meet between the alarm and a dream:
mine might be to cross the ocean again, or see airplanes flying backward,
or bombs fall upward, or homes given back, not this jittery skate along
the surface, legs splayed, listening to the noise of the clattering dishes
stored in the basement next to the expired survival kit and family photos,
the wool socks still in their packaging.

At least that's what I learned after hanging out at the taxidermist, even if
the futurologists keep telling us it's a new day—just look at the Batmobile
with dashboard aglow in green, carrying rescue gadgets and spewing fire

from its tailpipe while racing down a street of aluminum siding, gaps between the fences, and the omnipresence of need, i.e., I could leave here but I can't, and the larger the silence the more words it takes to fill it until you reach the ice cream stand at the end of the people mover where you waited for today's bonus flavor to be posted before moving down the terminal toward the next touchscreen, jabbing at it with your elbows after a retinal scan and private pat down, so it's fine with me if you want to say it's art, because that's also how we play the piano.

Then the dream in reverse is reversed again, and we look for shelter amid stutters and the river's swaying rushes as traffic steadily flows past, sometimes with a screech, sometimes with a whisper, but our immobile pony barely notices, attracted instead to the dandelions blooming under our feet and smoky clouds moving across the horizon in a narrative frequented by a history with flattened ears pressed against its head, which is why there are benefits to being able to breathe underwater, yet there were so many to call back we couldn't call them all, mouthed close to where we touch bottom while tipping a leaden scale, and there's some truth to this and some falsity as well, like a vending machine's robotic arm reaching into an empty row; at least we still have our lanterns and trail mix, and then there's always the mall—I can see the entrance from here, my head on a pillow made from discarded egg cartons painted to match a blue sky.

CAMPFIRES FOR DUMMIES®

A pile of aluminum cans will stymie most omnivores,
but not the trash heap that TV show invited me to.
                                                                                            Still,
not every loss is a departure,
                                        and I'm glad this love made it to summer,
                    the Italian ice running sticky between
your fingers like it can't help itself either,
                                            pawning a gold tooth,
as the darkest spot is marked by light,

and no one showed me that other than the light itself
                                                                           along with
the wreckage history piled high behind us.

Rain mutes the sounds from the street,
                                        except for ambulances
and a refrigerated delivery truck rumbling in front of Dunkin' Donuts,
            deer carcasses spilling from its side
                                              after the hunters
exceeded their quota while ignoring the court orders
because the law only applies to the hunters,
                                      never the prey.

The sea is in the apple.
Place one hand on the stomach,
                                  one hand on the heart.
Sophie chose purple flowers for the fire escape planting.
Snow fell in July,
                and we didn't even notice.
Air traffic controllers duck in their tower with each unscheduled landing,
the roar of the engines always in our ears,
                                      our ergonomic egg beaters
        at the ready.

AFTERNOON DELIGHT

Kiss the fuselage but ignore the paint job,
your first checked bag is always free.
After that you'll have to speak to a specialist
telling stories with an applicator brush that carves lines
into a barstool splitting the difference
    between soft, green fields and the places you've left,
      between the Wichita lineman and the message you sent,
    between history and more than 700 channels.

Just don't call it a hobby.
What does a lobster know way down there in the dark?
Our next vacation will be to the sand dunes.
Sometimes I don't think about anything except you,
like footsteps reaching a stair invented with
all the words we have for "and"

SONIC WARFARE

There's beauty on each page of that book,
    but that doesn't mean it says something pretty.
We upload images to a file named landscape,
    black sand spreading in every direction,
    almost like a flavor packet that might last forever
except if you give it a little pinch in the corner,
    it starts singing "Yankee Doodle Dandy"
    without knowing the words.
Otherwise, I'm here for the hobo snacks
    and forgetting old phone numbers.
Yet I'll always remember Daphne Chanute
    and the real estate agent who tried to sell me
    his boys' bunk beds because it's hard to die alone.

Chew through it and move on. Chew through it and move on.
You'll have to pay extra for unlimited data.
I took a bus to New Orleans for the weekend or else
    I steal the signal when it's my turn to speak.
The bones aren't ticklish; they're used for a cudgel,
    as various predators stir in the yard or go for a stroll
    after dinner.
I hit them with a half-finished can of Pepsi,
    like a kamikaze pilot aiming for a butterfly perched
    on the lip of a lifeboat.

That must be where my tube of ChapStick went after a night
   of rough kissing.

The wall is pockmarked with years of different pictures
   like a dog tugging the lining from a coat in its pantomime
   of skinned.
There are other times we've stepped outside the body,
   as the State aspires to transparent guardrails
   whereas the drunk unicyclist turns on a dime.
For now, let's assess the situation at the local Dairy Queen,
   and if we run out of ideas we can build another Death Star,
   this one even bigger and with one structural flaw obvious
   to any squid in a space suit.
I didn't need to do much research for that,
   but it made me shadowless in the fluorescents.

Yet the past is no indicator of future success,
   even for the jaw evolved to skim low to the ground.
I don't know if I'll eat another Blizzard with Captain Duffy,
   haphazard at the tiller, although there's one
   in my peripheral vision.
We return from vacation to find raccoons in the garage
   and the garden gnome sporting a chipped beard.
The remaining deliveries arrive by truck or train
   after being unloaded at the nearest port along with
   empty piñatas, friendship bracelets, methane,
   expired tricyclics, that painting of A-Rod as a centaur,
   vinyl bathmats, brine shrimp, and mood rings.

My only advice is never to play Pictionary
   with an ornithologist.
Otherwise, you're on your own in figuring out
   the irrigation system, knowing that I loathe arbitrary
   expressions of authority as much as you do.
There's freedom only in the present moment,

    however slack the lampshade.
I'll fix it in a minute with a spatula and rubber bands,
    or maybe just let the room slowly go dark.
One day I hope to find you, thin cursor parrying with white
    in the screen's soft glow.
We lead children by the hand away from danger.
The rest is mostly a story.

EVENING WEAR

Then the proud firefighter arrived
                        suffering from aphasia and packing
a few extra pounds for the winter.
                    We directed him to the frayed
speaker wire and clear blue flame
                        burning beneath a trapdoor in the heart.
The genie generator spigot is cracked,
                      so I set the phaser on stun and aimed it
at the sunset after we wiped the windows clean
                    but still can't see through them,
like a long, slow poke in the eye.
                        Forklifts and shopping carts roam
an enormous parking lot where we scooped
                    last season from a wishing well.
Inside, palm trees lean with a wind
                    scattering dental records and plutonium.
That's why I want to live next to a river,
                    maybe the one I saw from the laundry truck,
back flapping open at each stop.
                    Even a second job won't cover the payments.
Fighter jets strafe any survivors.
                    This village sits on the edge of a desert.
The art of magic can't set us free.
                    I'll be here at least until the diner closes,

blowing smoke through an accordion
                             while tinkling on the keys and their
consequence of the waltz.

LETTER OF THE LAW

We get the news faster from the animals
         alongside the slowly shifting seasons.
I also imagine a warehouse filled with
used office chairs, Wite-Out, and bandages
stacked to the ceiling,
because somebody has to pay these bills—
         someone other than the duck caller
and the locksmith who borrowed a nail gun
         to monogram our towels.

Afterward, we soaked our hand in warm, sudsy water
pending the results of a rabies test
and the point at which people get sick
         of the candidates.
There are doors that won't budge,
         however loud the knock,
but that just means
the party doesn't start until we arrive,
         RoboVac and margarita mix at the ready
while walking a waddling bulldog.

I wouldn't take any food inside the locker room
now that we're in an ongoing battle with gum disease,
         like a chef sampling too much of the cuisine.
My thinking might be digital,
but my head is full of sniffles,
         right-side up on the vertebrae this time
and made weightless after the space launch or sunk

so deep in a house gone aquatic I got nothing
        except gurgles and an ache when you leave.

My stop is next to the rockslide,
though thankfully not the cave in;
instead, we made ours from cardboard, masking tape,
        and fashion spreads ripped out of magazines
we found at the curb with a crack in the wing.
This is the cart for both groceries and laundry.
Soon, we'll all be working for the banks,
but we'll still have plenty to talk about
        and the chance to build campfires in the lobby.

GHOSTS THAT PURSUE US

We put in new floorboards after gravediggers destroyed
the old ones in overreacting to all this silence.
But each person is bigger than a story. Mudslides
washed cars off the road's edge.
                              That's where we found
our shoes wet in the tall grass. If we had a telescope,
we could see where we're going, as a star cloud finally
makes it to earth, drifting imperceptibly over the courthouse.

It looks like plastic, and it is. We hardly slept last night,
and now we're back in the office. Outside, trash trucks
haul away our lunch, and take the light with them too.
What's the advertisement that says
                            you can't stop with
a single bite? I wrote it for the desert. On the golf course
it's called taking a mulligan, except I haven't played since
tossing my clubs in the lake after missing a gimme.

Even then, I hated the fakery of it all. Now, I just don't
wear my glasses. Yet this video chat feature is going
to get me in trouble. I wait for the sun to set before deciding
which way is west.
　　　　　　　　　　The submarine that can also go on land
crushed a row of megaphones. That's okay with me,
because they're not creating the world we want, the one
where you aren't missing in it.

—*Marfa, Texas, July 2013*

PUBLIC HOTEL

We grope around in the cereal box to find the hidden prize,
but that's as close as I'll get to competitive eating.
At least it was choreographed so that we didn't feel lonely,
　　　knees gracefully breaking the water's chlorine surface
　　　　　while holding our breath underneath,
just as with the correct pressure,
　　　internal organs shift under muscles, fat, and ribs.
That's a form of journalism too,
　　　the endoscope imaging soft tissue, pollutants in the lungs,
　　　　　and flashing red lights minus their sirens.
Afterwards, I got a knuckle tattoo of a nuclear reactor cooling pool
　　　filled with the synchronized swimming team
　　　　　and a Sea World performance featuring the offspring of Shamu.
With the jet lag, I couldn't tell if the sun was rising or setting
　　　while wiring money home plus some to the river keepers
　　　　　or maybe toward the endings hummed in our ears.

But there still wasn't enough of the inheritance left
　　　to clean out the backyard,
slipping our fingers between the spokes that radiate
　　　from the heart's current location

and its boyfriend OPI Max Factor with painted toes.
Then the evergreens get ignored, except around Christmas,
as we live the dream in shopping bag exhaust
    billowing from the vents.
There's a rose garden commemorating that too.
The empty part of my desk kinda resembles a runway,
and life is an accumulation of little pieces,
    the dishes piled on the floor or the dents in the ceiling.
No wonder you went to bed early,
    even with all those channels to choose from;
I stayed up late plotting corporate takeovers.
A dog is also barking in this poem.

The next stop is the firefighter's ball,
    with complimentary tickets for the innocent civilians
    and a scolding from the meter maid for everyone else.
In other words, no parking on the dance floor.
That's easy for you to say after a trip to Jiffy Lube,
but my expectations are getting looser.
This poem casts a line to Saturn's shadowed half
    before heading back to the campaign trail,
    shaking hands and kissing babies,
only to end up buying rounds of drinks at the hotel bar.
I'll stick to the satellites and imperiled machines,
    along with a book by Uma Thurman's father,
    the noted Buddhist I keep bumping into at the laundromat.
I mean literally. I mean everything literally,
    because then it's like a flinty stone you can use to make sparks
    when you're alone, or in love, or it's getting dark, or you're a parent,
    or you're fucking sick to death of talk about the stock market.

We captured a sliver of it with a disposable camera,
and even that part got eclipsed by your thumb on the lens
    as the squirrels scampered beside us
    during our walk on the hospital grounds.
The illness rhymes with Fargo,

but that's not a riddle like when you can see the weather rolling across
    the horizon while standing at the kitchen sink,
        floral window valance blocking the top of what you know.
The heat is turned off at the elementary school
    for the entire winter recess,
        which means finding a family to take care of the class iguana,
and yet nothing messes up your flow like trying to coordinate that
    during a divorce.
At those moments, I aim to be smaller than a planetarium
    and obsessively fill this page's white space briefly turning a shade
    of mustard yellow matching the interior of a house I once lived in.
It's since been converted into a discount store
    for abandoned pets and fake ferns.

That might sound cruel,
but somewhere in the world right now there's a bomb being dropped
    or a rocket being launched.
The wind comes a little nearer to us when the front door slams shut
    or the tarp shakes loose, a torn corner left for shelter
    and the candidate's abs.
Schools of fish swim in the bay next to tankers and jet skis
    as anglers line the pier.
Next thing I knew Facebook told me it's your birthday.
I used to hang out in airports for fun,
but that was before 9/11 and surveillance everywhere.
I recently found the outtakes in a throw pillow—
    and to think, you said I was being paranoid!
I swore there was something pressing sharp against my head,
    although it might be a woodblock portrait of the ship's captain
    seeking to replace me.
In fact, I was once overtaken by doughnuts and fermented peaches.

Conjunction junction, what's my function?
Stabbing at the heart of it all.
I'm not entirely sure where the stain came from,
although I first saw it up there in the sky

where paratroopers descend into a hangover's lazy aim.
The bagels gave me a stomach ache inside the car's shiny silver finish
    with brown leather seats warming our legs and lips bit
    at the politician's fundraising dinner.
In the meantime, we'll be regularly monitoring the drones
    and tracking devices.
They know our names: spruce, pine, fir, cypress, cedar.
A squadron of cicadas chirps late into the night,
    leaving their shells behind for the casual observer,
just as language has effects, such as not always giving the correct change.
Poetry is a different kind of meaning.

So spackle the little holes after the pictures are removed.
The power cords snake around our feet.
There isn't a parking space within a mile of the stadium,
as crowds file in for the ceremony featuring crisp salutes
    and a dumpster filled with keychain whistles.
I ran a stop sign in my rush to get here.
The rest, as they say, is history, or one of them at least,
    with their various forms of public speaking,
including practicing our favorite pop songs in front of
    the bathroom mirror after a thorough application
    of peppermint body spray causing the neighbors to complain.
You can't send a text message from the upper atmosphere yet;
it takes a different kind of transmission where the weather balloons
    collect data on methane and acid rain.
I remember Three Mile Island and Love Canal.
I remember when we used to talk on the phone for hours.

Soft-haired Helen slept in Egypt while iron Troy burned.
It's not strawberry; it's strawberry-flavored, and everything is also
    something else.
That's the chorus, and you already know the drop.
There's an extra hour of daylight, so the ice cream stands are open late—
    burnt toast is this year's special flavor, with recipes sketched
    on the back of a napkin as ketchup dribbles down your shirt.

But I think it's still hockey season,
and there's pain at the pump,
    with fruit chews for consolation,
as we already begin to say good-bye, restless right there where we live;
    restless with this nation.
That's when I took on the voice of a time-keeper, skipping the coterie,
and your body couldn't be any warmer, the way some animals
    huddle together in the snow.
Soon it'll be spring, and we'll revise this as we go.

I painted the walls earth tones mixed with neon before turning on
    the black light for the gothic futurists harvesting fresh flowers
    and stainless steel placed in a diving bell shaped like a vase.
We wear it tighter than a cravat at the factory or a folk singer's
    cover version of "Stayin' Alive" with its dream of a better life.
But don't forget the crosswinds, the swirling 2×4s at a construction site
    where octopi work or serve as steak-knife swirlers.
The best I can do is capture the shadows with the sun right outside,
and if I'm lucky, I'll reach the bottom of this page without
    sending a check for the internet or getting a phone call
    from school or a letter from the government.
You were smart to become a novelist,
although there's no place for moralizing in art, only the blink of the present
    against a muddy scrim, like piling concrete blocks into a sifter
as a truck blocks local traffic while unloading its goods,
    horns honking for miles into the distance.

THE PLASTIC CHANDELIER

A quick shadow
    crosses sunlight
as we briefly turn off
    the electronic devices.
That was after we gave false names

  to the border patrol
and scratched constellations
  on the ceiling.

In my dream, I accidentally
  cut off a hearse,
then woke up
  with a pulled hamstring.
But that won't stop
  my holiday shopping
wherever dorsal fins
  slowly accumulate.

Getting up to see what kind of bird
  is making that noise,
I'm moving as fast
  as a forklift.
None of us are long
  for this earth,
so why do the banks
  keep closing?

The long drought honeycombed
  the landscape,
but the meat locker
  keeps peaceably humming
with scented candles and crew socks
  piled on top.
Gravity is its own form
  of undertow.

I missed your call on my way
  to the sawdust factory,
the first stop when
  buying a new home.
I tried to tune in

the traffic report,
    but only heard stories
of missing children.

I wrung out the collar after
    we got caught in the rain,
turning the sky into
    something we wear.
We took refuge
    in the airport casino,
and quickly lost the money
    for our ticket.

LAY OF THE LAND

The crystal vision sees everyone as ghosts
though not the lawn chairs they sit in
or the bamboo skewers charring on the portable grill,
which are gifts from the decaying world.
Yet I'm not certain I'll be able to make it without you.
The rest can be found online or at Walmart,
especially now with my phone telling me where to go.
It asks me where I am at each moment.
But I moved to this city to be anonymous when I want,
to collect the modest roses.

We can evacuate either orderly or in a panic.
Tapping out complex number sets
while waiting in line at the train station bathroom
keeps me sane and distracted.
At least that's what the neighborhood vet said
after overrunning the police lines.
Then the judges decide who made up the law,
as I fall behind on my payments.

In hindsight I probably didn't need that many glue guns,
even if at the time they seemed like a steal.

I'm inside backing up my photos and listening to
hourly updates on the prison break
after exchanging uniforms with the guards and feeding
barbed wire to the latest aggregator.
A convenience store clerk cleans the display case
with paper towels and Windex®.
That's a lot of effort to go to for a strip of beef jerky,
although I'm glad you think it was worth it.
The shining city on the hill caught fire in our dreams,
so let's build the animal shelter closer to the woods.

DRY GOODS

You could be any number of places at once.
This time
        it just happens to be on the fire escape
   with the wisteria, pigeon shimmy,
                         and constant machine rumble.
It's like it keeps happening in threes:
you   me   and the ghost sitting next to us.
How many ways can I say that I'm not a morning person?
I'm closer to the other side
                  of a new day.

Astronauts accrue massive frequent flyer miles
whenever they escape transmission range.
Otherwise,
      this world is the inside of steel or
glued-on floor tiles
              digging out from under
   the commands.

                  I once signed for a mortgage;
now I can barely finish this word search.
The playground is painted in primary colors.
Five hundred years on this continent,
and almost every forest
                  has been razed.

I've seen meds work for certain people,
slowing down the blink.
                  At the waterfall house
we go to bed early.
That's when the turtles practice underwater somersaults
in a pond of Listerine.
                  We started our small compost heap
    with used hairnets.
Later we added scraps of food and candidate yarn,
while bootleggers videotaped the movie
                  right off the screen.

Terrariums don't have stars where you fell,
    only tiny signs obscured by spongy moss.
Upon splashdown,
                  the ocean was choppy with a slight tug
of undertow,
            and back on the beach we lost
control over the Cheez Whiz.
The automated features didn't make it any easier
after we spent hours setting up
                  an account.

Anything to squeeze some extra money out of you,
even if it's only a blimp bringing more frozen catfish.
Yet all that hurt can start to sharpen.
                  Just don't
    lift the lid on it.
            Instead, Facebook will tell you when.

I'm not sure I even live here, a short walk from
the Williamsburg Bridge.
                         Not no there there,
but too much there there. Is that how I got picked
to be staff meteorologist
                         for the rainmaker?

FAIRYTALES OF THE LATE HOLOCENE

The dictionary doubled
as a cookbook after
we forgot to restock
the pantry while
recalling the good times
or an extended bout
of eye rolling.
Some stuff makes
your head hurt
before you even hear it.
On cold days,
I see some people wear
earmuffs over their hat.

It'll be light out
for a few more minutes.
Remind me when
you're coming home.
I fill my wicker basket,
and it's not enough.
Medical supplies stored
in a makeshift tent
travel the world
on a freighter carrying
bicycle parts and

striped beach balls
tumbling into the sea.

It used to be called
the rabbit hole;
now it's known
as the market and a
bent pocket mirror giving
every user a unibrow.
The first key to love
is patience,
but it's hard
to sit still in the dark,
so say hello again
to the bass. And what's
a pantry, anyway?

INTELLIGENCE GATHERING

The bees came back to make their honey
which for us means staying slightly faster
        than the police. These are the birdcall
scrapyards rearranging the mental furniture one stick
        of kindling each. I didn't invent
the quiet storm, but I used to tune in with
        play and record buttons at the ready.
Now we put the crown on scramble and lite bites on repeat.

The bat must have flown in via the chimney
        and digital effects. There's a lot of shouting
on that channel and in that house, yet only
        a little in this poem. We leave a porch light on
for the drones airlifting takeout, surgical strikes,

and a stopwatch used to time a standing mile
        for the car on cinderblocks.

The instruction manual arrived as suddenly salad,
yet nothing's worse than the holier-than-thou routine,
        the spilled drink when we weren't
even thirsty, demoralizing the clubhouse mystique,
just as a little bit of water always flows over
        the dam. That doesn't make me feel any better
living downstream, though it certainly reassures the canoe.

Otherwise, maybe it's best to pack a sandwich
for this wage race to the bottom, this history
        as pastiche, just as every day I'm hustling or
shuffling, so call me maybe. A pilot aborted
the landing while sending text messages to
        the clouds, as a thinning ozone warms up
the livestock auctions.

We stand directly beneath the engines, though if
you listen closely you can hear photosynthesis too,
or maybe it's the baby in the TV commercial
        pushing online trading.
I'm just trying to sit still for a minute while also
        hanging the drapes, because everything
out the window seems far away. That's also the name
of the bar's signature drink.

Wherever there's a popcorn machine decorating
a weathervane, we'll be sure to find it.
In fact, we'll treat it the way a dog might,
        tongues wagging, then inexplicably bury it
only to dig it up again dented and rusted next summer.
It's better than being strapped to the roof of
the family sedan with the trickle-down voodoo
        we'll have to wash away later.

My patience has lasted for decades. A box of old
electronics sits on a shelf in the closet.
One day, I might value everything I've forgotten,
but not when there's a battleship in the harbor filled
      with dangerous alien invaders. I wish they'd
take me away instead of ending up in my head.
But you won't force a confession out of me,
      at least not yet.

I deleted that last tweet and wrapped it in a bandage,
      along with hair extensions, Almond Joy packaging,
      train wrecks, sunshine, coffee, and pudding.
Kindred spirits sing from the pine trees. There's a type
      of understanding in which there's no understanding.
Cowboys are doing that rounding-things-up thing again,
as the tombstone turnstiles bang against our waist.

REVENGE OF THE CHEERLEADERS

I once was a plastic surgeon for the pot roast,
      although that history has become a blur to me,
as if Tom Cruise's spaceship
                flew through it.
I mean, I'm neither a celebrity nor in rehab,
      but that's what this poem is about.
I'll finish the rest of it when I'm back
                  from kneecap replacement
      after refusing to kiss the ring.

Everyone wears a uniform:
            mine flaps its arms
when a string gets pulled;
      yours stomps a foot.
Almost on cue, a herd of caribou migrates across permafrost.

The larger ones knock over whole cities,
        but no one noticed now
                that the architecture
is mostly virtual while still fueled by carbon
        as we make small talk about the weather
            or the death of the organist.

Yet I can tell you think deeply about things,
        sitting quietly in your seat
                as we speed through
the landscape wondering how did this crow end up
        so far into the desert,
              its wing
        a black blossom in the corner of my eye.
Next I know,
        I'm having to justify my timeline,
such as marching a clown brigade into the Grand Canyon,
        with our makeup running in rivulets
            like a novice willow.

So spare me your fruity drinks;
                the best way to take it
        is through the mainline.
I haven't even mentioned the Kardashians or my participation
        in a little something I like to call
                fireside follies,
which involved you taking a baseball bat
                to the entire apartment
while I looked at family albums.
                Felt good, though, didn't it?
Anything to get me out of here after hauling in enough sand
to reconstruct the beach
            destroyed by winter storms.

FIELD GUIDE

Back in those days,
    I didn't document much: now there's
a constant threat of pepper spray in the air.
Not coincidentally,
    it's the holiday season again with its rows
of green and red stripes and outrage.
My pet tropical fish, Pinky,
    has no one to bully in its tank, so together
we practice the old sleep-with-your-eyes-open trick.
I like whatever reminds me of time.
After that, I like whatever
    reminds me of love.
The rainmaking machine needs a new compressor
    and its prior memory erased.
Condos rise on what was once a distant piece
    of swampland, but I'm still out of the loop since
losing the room number for the wind-shear meeting
    announcing the caretaker's role.
You tuck your knees up when you go to sleep,
    and emails are left unanswered.
We take a chill out of the air with Jolly Ranchers,
    then wipe down the countertops
with bath towels and salt,
    as the truck stop began to feel more like home.
The rest of the meat is served on skewers;
but if you want ruthless,
    you could try the dining car.
That's not exactly a ringing endorsement,
    listening to the playground fill up with kids.
The rest of the sky is streaked with contrails heading
    anywhere out of this world.
Yet I can't go back,
    even if it's still with me,
and no one except you can do the roar.

When the messages arrive,
    they arrive without measure—
rattle of glasses in the cupboard,
a television floating close to shore.
I'll just take the check, please, after dumping
    everything else in the category called hunger.

LOST IN THE GARDEN

ECHOES

We won't get out of here alive
while waiting to strike an iceberg
    already stroking the hull.

Those were the mornings
    you could barely get out of bed,
a balloon's thin string clenched
        in your fist.

Inevitably you have to let it go
    like fireflies and their glow.

   *

The donkey knows the trail from repetition
    and a stick, from the dust kicked up
by the tanks at Mount Rushmore.

Cities in revolt.
        My face is a screen.

Children climb higher in the trees.

I want it to be bigger than me.

   *

There's static in every transmission.

The headlights are stubby in the darkness and fog.

We keep our dresses and divorce in the basement.

Who's going to fix the sky?
It is broken
              and so are our heads.

   *

You have the words for safekeeping;
I have the songs playing on my phone.

We lost years to the war, as we pass
           from shadow to light
    and back again,

hungry the entire trip.

You can reach me where I've never been,
the smiles stuck between my teeth.

   *

crooked mouth   can't fly right

Violence fills the bandwidth.
There are more animals than trough.

We build our boat out of flames—
                     all flying things fleeing up ahead of us.

       Instead, I'm going under.

This poem is the compost for my joy,
planter tipped over, dirt spilling
                     on the floor.

   *

Fire needs oxygen,
    yet the room is running out of air.

The old ways are dying.   The new ones too.

I live half of my life online
         and the other half on a rented wheel
that deducts the charges from my credit card.

   *

The heart has neurons.

I am lost in the networks.

Night falls quietly around us.

The house was mute today.

*

No flags anywhere ever.

I hope we meet far from here.

The whole desert might shift,
but it's one grain of sand at a time—
each one a universe
             filled with a universe
                        filled with infinite sails.

*

a break in the clouds   foam on the sea

Some ducks swim in a row,

        but I digress.

I gave my answers in a sputter.
The sense we make is provisional.

*

We woke up early next to a lake
where a few stars twinkled
                on its dark surface

An angry dog pulls the leash taut.

The museum of the heart should be free,
but this country is built on cruelty.

*

Green vines weave through a trellis
the way we use a barrette
                to pin back our hair
and put one thing next to another
                until the links exceed us.

You called it a homecoming,
                but this isn't our land.

*

A part of my tooth broke off,
                but I kept on chewing.

Location on.   Camera on.   Microphone on.

You said it would be good for the brand.
Please don't take advantage of the junkie.

Where the computers are made,
                the factory was like a city.

The virtual architectures are designed to contain.
The wolves are also in the house.

*

Midnight of the idols.

Ghosts wander the halls
                of your name.

Another day without you or me either,

                      hints of blue.

Poppies grow in memory's soil.

I'm trying to break into film.

    *

If it wasn't for the refinery,
                      I could see clear to the horizon.

Plastic got loose in the food chain,
                      and so did we.

It's hard to sprint in clown shoes.

Not everything floats in the ocean.

Although I've removed
            a bunch of words,
        I'm not getting any closer to the tree line.

    *

I sometimes have trouble making the pieces
        go together,
yet they're part of a whole
                like weeds to the whacker.

Everything outside is inside too.

No more stories.   So many guns.

The elevator went crooked to the top,
which is also what happened to our money.

    *

Summer crept up on us
        after a winter   with so much dying
we were almost hesitant
        to step into the light

                until the fires started burning.

    *

The small songbirds don't care where we go,

just as it's the nature of the horizon
                            to always recede

where we didn't leave a trace
                other than in the soil and stars

and the sunsets are beautiful
                through the pollution.

    *

I can barely drive a plow,
                which made the crop circles
        illegible to the aliens.

Later, we pulled over
        on the side of the road

to try to get some sleep
                       but forgot the notebook
     for our dreams.

*

one side has bombs   the other has rocks

An oil spill soaked into the beach
where the clouds invent their own shapes.

Do we come before the earth
                        or after it?

Language takes scissors to the landscape.

I needed a cleanup on every aisle
when my heart started leaking.

*

In the morning
                   our faces walked through the new spiderwebs.

We were happy to be alive,
         to return to the river.

*

Sweet love.

Summer settles into stillness
while cruise ships

                drift in the harbor.

      My semaphore unfurls a roll of toilet paper
      along the shore;

      my semaphore waves the bouquet of flowers
      you gave me.

   *

When I lived in the desert
                I whispered to stones,
     then put them back where I found them,
                               like a god did to me.

Some days are a stutter   others are a flow.

I listen to the ghosts speak.

Poetry is not efficient.

   *

bristlecone pine   giant sequoia

At night,
               we listen to the drone of cicadas
and trucks passing
          on a nearby highway.

It feels like I haven't been home in years.

The impossible is not only that.

*

Some people return from the dead   and some don't
no matter what the epigraph says

or the message in a green bottle
that washes up on shore
                      where every world is a shipwreck.

*

We also call
them beginnings
like when I reach the end
of this page
and nothing's left
except a voice
asking where
to go next,

gravel underfoot,
blinking satellite overhead.

        The water is disappearing from the river.

I stand corrected.
I sit corrected too.

*

The screen is continually flickering,
                            but we don't see it.
The image wishes death to the human
as the iconoclasts knew.

Anxious language is tighter.

My head like a rack of lamb.

That's bad.   That's like the news.

    *

It snowed for the entire drive,
        yet it still felt familiar
with all the other routes unavailable
        and the pharmacy closed.

So many no's became like a yes,
or maybe that's what's known
                      as acceptance

and discovering how common the willow tree is.

We'll all be leaving soon.

    *

We spend Sunday getting ready for work on Monday
when we'd rather be knitting or climbing a tree

because you only get one life
and sometimes less than that.

        Saltwater corrodes the speaker wire.

My swollen lip has a swollen lip,
                and that's what's talking now.

*

Some people grease the wheel with money,
                               others with butter.

The pets have names similar to the humans.

Most days are stolen from us.

The monuments are a testimony to slaughter.

*

I ride on a cargo ship.

       We fill out the forms with false names
before the cops arrive,
                forgetting that they're already here
ready to make up the rules
                like a rancher to the land.

A hornet jabs a neon sign with its stinger,
        two buzzings,

     plus another inside my head.

*

Time also goes in circles

      like the hawk above a field
      where mice are the moments.

Who knows what's living
                     in the back of the yard?

Leave the kitten a little milk on the plate.

       There are some things I'd rather forget.

    *

I turned the popcorn machine to soft,
and it started making marshmallows.

I'm only crying on the outside;
                     inside, it's even worse,
      like something metal
                 left in a heat wave.

Toxins build up in the blood.

I will try to be a light   in my own darkness—

       just don't let the priests know.

    *

A dog barks at the footsteps in the hallway.

This poem is like throwing a party
                     for the ants.

What's one line in a whole book?   Everything.

My only symptom is a fever.

We managed to get two on a unicycle
        but crashed it soon.

Defeat smells   like fear in the present age,
            like flashing a gun on New Year's Eve.

   *

Rain didn't end the drought.
Some called it Babylon in the heat.

Everyone's got a hustle.

My computer is good for gaming.

The human is a virus too.

   *

I sat on the porch shucking corn
before smiling
            for my school portrait,
emotional support dog
        tucked under my arm
while keeping the politicians at bay
                with a stick.

Hobos float by on salvaged boats
        soaked like bandages
                    dropped in a puddle.

*

We duck the kicks while hand-cranking
        a makeshift Ferris wheel
and its two seats that don't peek
                above the gas station's roof.

That's what it was like to live in that house,
        emergency lights flashing
                through the window.

*

The road unwinds in front of us,
                even though we're sitting still,
      the trees glitching at higher speeds.

The sunlight adjusts its pixels.

I don't want to be absorbed in one story
        like the UFO hidden in a comet's tail
        or a cigarette and a drink.

All the transactions are visible on the blockchain.

*

A pyramid of ketchup bottles slides off a palette.
Gray scratch-off specks ended up in the bed.

Of course the warranty is expired.

We watch it all on a screen
                or many of them.

The city is an archive,
                     yet change only happens
    in the streets.

   *

All the names are made up, anyway.

The me is small flotsam to the beach,
    the you is the pail,
         and love is the scoop.

Where there isn't love,
predators' wings blot out the sun.

Quiet rain come down on me.

PUNCTURE WOUND

We don't need another winter around here
    when our dreamboat is better known
as tubing. There's rain in the sky
    and in my heart, but I'd rather change
the place names, remove the hands
    from the clockfaces even if the destination
feels so far away to our fleet
    of invisible scooters until it looms up
to greet us, vinyl siding peeling off the facade
    like a cigarette for the dying.

We're good at finding the symptom
    but not the cure after we called the health line
and reached a satellite in orbit,
    or tried the request line and connected

with someone's dad. I would stop writing
    if the world got better but not if I did
after leaving a pie on the windowsill
    for the hobos except the mayor ate it,
then put a throat lozenge in its spot
    that a bird flew away with,

just as my gift card is for another gift card,
    which is kind of how the stock market works,
so please show me the nearest door.
    It was easier when we wore pelts,
not these scuffed collars for our positions
    in service next to a display case
filled with beach balls, insulin, and guns.
    What is our inheritance? Face down
on the hood is what the police teach.
    Next it will be the machines.

FOR LOVE AND MONEY

We flew the coop only to land on a dinner plate,
carving knife at the ready where our necks are thinnest,
but at least no one smiled at us this time or got out
the party platter with pale roses circling its rim.
This meal will be over soon, at least until the next one,
as our list of demands gets turned into email spam
after filling out the spreadsheet while Martians send
their signals through the Wi-Fi.

Next thing we knew we were shopping in the suburbs,
which was almost worse, the air conditioner broken
and the car smelling of sweat and strong cologne
as an empty water bottle rolls around on the floor.

I'll take a quiet room and a few ice cubes, or a fireplace
and lighter fluid, because this world will consume itself
one tank of gas at a time or one Dixie Cup full of piss,
but I'll never whistle it.

A tractor trailer jackknifed with a load of medical supplies
and my Netflix subscription. I found a goat keeping cool
in the bathtub after it ate my curling iron and a plastic fork
lost behind the toilet years ago. It's a good thing
the Terminator ended up at the foundry; I wish I could claim
the same about my breakfast before I dumped it out
on the Cape where it mixed with an oil spill spreading up
the East Coast from Florida to Boston Common.

The hot box is metaphorical after we switched the string
of LED lights to yellow and enjoyed the mellow vibe.
Bodies might seem inefficient with their frequent leakage,
but that's synergy. This isn't a hopscotch tournament,
so I'd better get focused. It's called a disruption of service,
and I wish it would happen more. No wonder we preferred
to remain on the ferry, coconuts rotting on the shore
where a few crabs scurry.

Sometimes success is not having any, so you can bite
my lip a little bit when you kiss it, close my hand
gently around a fragile egg. Thick green of the season
makes me want to meet a tree, wrap my arms
around its bark and squeeze the way caulk does to a seam
or nightmares to a dream when the dark room glints
with ghosts, with frosting on the walls and creeping insects,
with the humming bones of my skull.

I can already tell that guy is going to be hostile, and he
hasn't even started talking. It's either a hammock or a canoe,
a faint breeze or a chemical leak. I don't know what's in
a whoopie pie, but I like the name, even when the unhappiness

is palpable. That's when Siri asked me, What's the deal
with emotions? A pair of sparrows splash in a puddle
while we patiently wait our turn after our pencil collection
got used for kindling, and it isn't even winter.

You told me I'd feel better in the morning, but I'm starting
to have my doubts. Where is that tumbleweed going?
Ten years at the same company and I never got a raise;
come to think of it, I never got a paycheck either.
I painted the boat blue so I can always see the bottom,
except tonight when the stars shine their dangling wishes,
catchy like a cold sneezing into a tissue even though
it's hot girl summer on the radio.

What will we do for love and money when nothing's certain
around here with all the lost jobs and pets wandering off?
One thing that never changes are the bedspreads
at the motor lodge. We nickname them Itchy and Scratchy,
although they'd probably do in a pinch for a pup tent
on Everest. I am so far from home. My friend the sign painter
got laid off while I was on my way to see Dua Lipa.
Let's just say it's been that kind of day.

SONG TO THE CYPRESS

The sky is filled with invisible things,
                          yet I can see the wrecking ball clearly.
We used a meat thermometer
                  when the medical one broke,
     but didn't know where to insert it.
Fish scales can't measure the flop
                  after everything falls apart.
That's when we went viral
                  along with a video of a dancing houseplant

            as algorithms drive the meaning,
although I'm hoping it's only the caffeine
                      that's making me sit here and shake.

The feedback loop is mostly static
                      and drives the boats from shore.
I'm still waiting for the technology that lifts us up,
                      as the cameras see me on the inside too.
These words have got me around the neck
                      like seeds in a sparrow's tiny talons
        before making their way to the landfill
along with whatever couldn't be included
                      in the estate sale and the backlash
        known as Tony Orlando and Dawn
because I'm not interested in nostalgia
                      when the past was designed to hurt.

The railroad crossing gate bounces off the car's hood
                      on a trip to the vet
        and then the florist.
Anyone could come through the window,
                      so like me that flock is getting its waddle on.
I have almost always lost what I have loved,
                      but sometimes it was also my fault,
        either too close or too far away,
and that's a bigger story about the world
                      that I don't know how to tell.
Some bugs just want to cling to the screen.

SHALLOW WATER SKIFF

I'm having trouble getting started
  but not ending.
Sometimes you have to walk away

from it all.
No more drama
   yet there was still plenty of it,
so toss me a paddle for steering clear
   of the cemetery in a flood plain.
I don't know if it's cold or just me.
I squeezed out a word or two
   amid the shouting,
like the doll's house around my neck
   where each room contains
   its own removal.
No wonder there's a red light
   on the alarm clock,
although not on the storm moving in.
Nothing should be the same after this.

DATA DUMP

1)

The latest charges will appear on your next bill
as well as the side of a cop car. We left our mattress
in the rain during these thunderstorms in summer,
so now you can call me soggy in time for my nap

with a gentle breeze blowing the leaves around me
while forgetting that insomnia during the day
is anxiety clattering like a tray full of knives dropped
on the kitchen floor along with a foreclosure notice.

I can't anymore. The wheels turn so slowly you can see
the spokes, just as we flicker a bit in the darkness.
My head is filled with coupons and breath mints,
with soap dishes and a microwave used to reheat

the pie served with humble, a napkin, and spackle
as if all of these holes will ever be filled except where
stardust squeezes through them like honey from
that little plastic bear or your basket of soft peaches.

I save an hour a day for weaving, but it unravels
each night except for the corner with our names in it
because where's the new in our language after
onion rings left greasy O's on the paper tablecloth

like silent screams or the parting shot of the coral
that sees everything is interconnected, including you,
loose shoelace, fraying around the edges with
each step, and believe me, I know the feeling.

2)

We drove into the forest and only emerged after dark
with the bats and an electronic ticker tape
endlessly scrolling alongside my jaw. If no one
is allowed on the dance floor, then isn't it just a floor?

So I filled it with flowerpots that blink on and off
in tandem with a strobe light, the way we dance
when you're not looking or behind a fog machine
when you are, as we hide the sun in the lion's mouth.

Is it a blizzard or a heat wave? One day the human
will be over. Before that happens, I need to finish
my homework on the mysteries of Atlantis:
one version features Jason Momoa with his shirt off,

although I'm from the generation of Lisa Bonet.
Not even a god can save us or the flying fish
briefly rising above the surface to squint at the glare
or escape the terrors pursuing them from the deep.

I might be New Jersey, but soon I'll be moving down
to Florida. Don't tell me things are getting better
when there's spit from the choir flying all over
and trouble following Tony Stark wherever he goes,

except that the longest lines are at the food bank.
I might sometimes lose hope, but I'm never cynical.
What else is being sold? Cherries and a rash.
A trippy aquarium. Evening on the horizon.

MORE FIRE

There are as many bugs here as words in my head,
and they both create the same din.
The meds make it better until the next big wave,
which is why I can mostly sympathize
with your desire to blow it all up and start over.
Yet how many beers are you going to spill on me first
after the Styrofoam cooler drifted out to sea
along with a black paddleboat the local goths like to rent,
empty tube of sunscreen on the seat?

The carousel stopped spinning and its lights blinked off.
I got in my car and drove past the moon,
stopping along the way for various craters,
although I didn't need to leave home for that.
What else should I be doing—shopping?
I'd rather make some bubbles,
so come find me at the bake sale, I mean, book table
where I ride the gravy train with a little ladle
while humming a choo choo tune.

The big men get the money first,
while the rest get a roll of cheap paper towels,

and not even the thick kind,
but the version that shreds when wiping up my lunch.
As the oceans rise during global warming,
seaworthy takes on new meaning.
I have tried to push back against the flood,
and now my shirt is off the shoulder,
stretched and droopy like this simile.

Al Gore may have invented the internet,
but I invented the dunk tank with clown makeup optional
or boardshorts hemmed below the knee
except the tightening is in my chest.
I'm not a hot mess, although sometimes I'd like to be.
Little blue bird might say tweet,
but I've never seen a hummingbird take a nap,
just act cranky and strange,
like polar bears watching their ice floes shrink.

Afterward, I gave myself the worst haircut,
but what can you do when you can't see the back?
Disease arrived with the covered wagons
and millions of buffalo skulls in heaps
as the smell of sulfur trails behind the hunters.
Please don't call me a throw pillow on Muscle Beach
because I'm already spread a bit thin
like my grandmother's Velveeta on Triscuits.
It is a very bad world we live in.

FUNNEL VISION

If there's a Cheeto left in the sofa,
      that beagle will find it.
The container ships bring me more
      stuff to throw away.

The only poor people traveling to Mars
	will be the ones cleaning out
	the dirty spacesuits,
but my portable jetpack won't get me there.
Neither will this shaky card table,
	although the good news is that it floats,
and I will cling to it if need be until the waters recede,
and I don't mean from the beach
	or this thirty-second ad before Siri
	whispers good night in my ear
	as I fall asleep.

They used to be known
	as the captains of industry;
now we call them the destroyers of everything
	that hides in the forest.
Wallpaper may be making a comeback,
	yet it won't cover up the holes
	where your fist went through
when violence is the lesson
	this country teaches.
So much already gone.
We escaped to the candy aisle
	where the bags keep getting bigger,
	along with jars of CBD gummies
we chew by the fistful every time we listen
	to the news.

It's hard to calm down
	when the leash is frayed
	and dragging along the ground
as the police strap on their riot gear
	after someone stole a set
	of chrome wind chimes from Home Depot.
I would have preferred a riding mower
	for getting around town,

except the DMV tells me
        it isn't street legal
but that it's fine to drink alone
        with the curtains closed and hall light
            shining on a pair of muddy boots
because it's been raining for days,
        and on the inside too.

Cool air in through the nose,
        warm air out.
Some days the pain was so thick,
        I couldn't see through it.
Fill all the guns with water
        and aim them at the clown's mouth.
No amount of isometrics
        is going to keep away the bullies,
and it's hard to imagine that the world
        is running out of sand.
Otherwise, I'm not sure
        what you were thinking,
although I'm guessing it wasn't about me,
        which is fine because life moves on,
            and so did we.

JAWBONE OF AN ASS

Everything is a simile. My loose change
fell between the cushions, and now

I can't pay the meter after being hired
to take the smell out of eggs and inspect

the ports, beginning with Houston.
Instead, it's endless debates about the same

as the virus spreads like a caption
bigger than the photo of us trying

to bivouac a portable submersible
through the pines of the Shenandoah.

I won't get there, but maybe you will,
as I take my rest under this tree,

older than all of us. Sunlight flares
in the camera lens. There are more

important things than my convenience,
but I still need to get to the store before

it closes, pushing my borrowed
shopping cart downhill until I reach

a full head of steam and nothing
can stop me except that oncoming car.

A red-tailed hawk watches from a branch.
I can still be found. It's always snowing

somewhere, even if only on TV, although
the remote control gets sweaty in my hand

when I'm beneath the pink fleece blanket.
Robots will eventually open every

time capsule; mine contains a can
of corn because history has mostly been

a series of slaughters, a row of bulldozers
ready for whatever's left over.

My backyard rocket ship got me as high
as the clothesline. After that, it's back

to quarantine while the camera outside
the bank keeps a close eye on the street.

The algorithms led me to this—a shattered
collarbone and empty bag of dog treats.

I could be more specific, except that something
doesn't feel right, and it's called the world.

The collision alert system didn't save us.
The tow truck backed right up to the house.

THE FOUR SEASONS

The hay in the barn is full of rot,
and so is this soda you left
on the counter, although the world
is still heating up, and I don't mean
the texts you sent at a quarter after one
in the morning. I mean my fire in the forest,
my vehicular damage, the little cracks
in my face. It's hard to live in the country.
Charlie with the Chow Chow is dead.

We fill the shopping cart with clothes,
although you can call them girdles.
My summer house is the same
as my winter one, but every spring
I like to lay an egg and forget about
the planting while hiding from my bank.
I'm in love with a robot after we kissed

in the fade, even if breakups make me
both sad and full of wonder.

That's when you're on your own
with one taco per serving, a side
of guac, and oil spattered from a pan.
The steel is cold to the touch,
and so is the promise ring.
When it's silent, I can hear the changes—
some are this close and some far away
like a song heard in a grocery store
or an alarm clock when you're hungover.

Each equinox is a rip in the fabric;
each solstice is a hole. I'm not
the highest in the room, but I'm stolen
in the gloaming and coming back to you
because the sun still peeks through,
enables updates and a slowly ripening
pile of apples. They've been replaced
by anime, and so have I.
We are our screens' dreams.

SPLASHES AND PLOPS

The view through the telescope is the same as the microscope
when everything splinters into light. Until then, I'll need
to purchase inner ear insurance after I got the wobbles
one stanza at a time. Reddit says that only old people
eat Fig Newtons, and I didn't know if this was true
or if Crimea will eventually be swallowed by the sea,
but the aging hippies across the street seem harmless;
they even let me borrow their Subaru and a trowel I wiped clean
on my jeans before uprooting tubers while the engine block

took hours to cool from driving around all day in the heat.
You've got the EMT on speed dial after a bidet malfunctioned
at the space station on a journey to explore another planet
the way an amateur motocross team treats soft earthen berms.
In other words, to destroy it. I can also be more specific,
although I'm not going to run to retrieve the ingredients
with this toothache that Super Glue isn't fixing.

Is there a point to this story? Nothing moral. I like splashing
in the puddle with the other birds. Do you think you're
better off alone? Save me from the nothing I've become.
Rain is falling again today, and you are still so far away
as the quiet amplifies once the chainsaw stops chewing.
I've almost graduated from college, but what's the rush?
I made a Tumblr of tumbleweeds, but no one found it funny.
It's okay to lay your burden down for a moment.
The keys are on the counter. Sometimes I just need a hug
and a burrito, maybe "Mean" Joe Greene's jersey to go
with a Coke. I am a clutter, so give me a paper towel
for the disaster and I'll make a sail with it and get as far
as last call sitting on a barstool at the nearest Fuddruckers
and wearing a disposable mask like a smudge. Don't tell me
I can do better while the juggled meat cleavers clatter
on the kitchen tiles. Like Frogger, I choose the log.

CAPILLARY

My head is the caption for my neck.

Who taught the bees how to be dirty?

I couldn't finish the plate of profiteroles.

We were drunk all the time, but then it wasn't fun.

Dungeons & Dragons is a lot of sitting around and talking.

There's now a mass shooting almost every day.

We are part of the fungus and part of the machine.

America has the biggest hogs.

How do you know when an iguana is sick?

My campaign donation is an empty shoebox.

The farm brings its harvest to the city.

This is not the language of utility or futility.

The surf 'n' turf gave me hoof-and-mouth disease and a sunburn.

We made a person with a computer.

What does a bank want with a house?

Like a tree, I am full of daydreams.

Slytherin or Gryffindor?

The neighbors won't stop yelling.

We threw the car keys into the lake.

This is a brutal country founded on genocide and slavery.

It can be hard to look with hope to the future.

We are trying to turn the world on its head.

The mist lingered for days.

DIRECT DEPOSIT

The light shines on us at a different angle
beneath the surface of the lake
with its quieter static, its lens
turned inside out placing the stars
beneath our feet, like runny eggs
or something better than Father's Day,
ham steak, drizzling rain, a stoved boat.
Ouch is right, although it's frequently
much worse. We breathe the contrails
or poke our head through smoke rings
asking: Where do we go from here?
I'll take one of these without a map—
just don't try to tell me it's a cookie
when all I see are jagged edges
and rooftop visions pushing
a shopping cart through mud.

That's why I brought a broom
and a shammy. Feel free to make up
the rest. When we were kids
we rolled a trash can down the hill.
Now I fill it up each week, as the sun
scolds us from behind the day.
How do you keep a hula hoop clean
when our waists are always so dirty?
We sleep with the language
and eat it too, though that's no excuse
for going through my phone
the way I used to do with yours,
coming home to something smaller,
like a character reduced to a crawl.
From outside the house,
we slip a note under the door.

LOCATION SCOUT

The wind will still blow in the trees
  long after we've left this place
    with our households on our backs
      and fanny packs in the desert
    for when the money gets sweaty
  in our waistbands.
Just don't call me Little Miss Effervescent
  or Mr. Efficiency.
    I'd rather extrapolate the mumblers
      than the numbers,
    but first I need
  to do the laundry
after you left enough hair
  in the bathtub drain to make
    a crooked toupee,
      like forgetting to clear
    your browser after spending
  an hour on Pornhub
and eating a bag of SunChips.

For now the rain is mostly free,
  but soon you'll have to pay for that too
    and someone to clean it.
      I forget what a map looks like,
    except for the gates and their keepers.
  No wonder we got so overheated
at the rodeo
  with the cowboy's lasso tight
    around our heels
      since the clowns
    no longer protect us.
  Where did my wand go?
I saw the best minds of my generation
  posting on Facebook.

   Somebody please help the child
     stop crying.
   There's only so much
 a person can do to avoid
the drama but not the heartache.

That's why from now on
  it's Ranch dressing on everything—
    life's too short for crunchy.
     The spiders could take over
    if they ever get organized,
  and you could say the same for us.
The harbor is so polluted
 that no fish swim in it,
   but occasionally a passenger will fall off
    the back of a cruise ship.
   Like Lil Peep, sometimes I don't want
 to leave my room.
Today is a different story
  after Thomas Morton set up a Maypole
   and invited the neighbors.
    Emptying your head
   is the easy part;
  getting rid of the cops
is much harder.

I watch my life pass on a small screen
  along with Boomer memes
    and inspirational sayings such as,
     If the mouth of the cookie jar is big enough,
    stick both hands in.
  But pretty much everything
makes me uncomfortable these days,
  including this fake bacon
   on a wedge of iceberg lettuce
     grown hydroponically next to

   the marijuana and daisies,
    the lavender and oiled beefcakes.
The architecture is wobbly.
 I don't always know
   where I'm going
    or where I've been
   while following the river's course
 known as anywhere
away from here.

EVER GIVEN

Delivery trucks swarm the roads
the way toilet paper flushes.
I drank Irish coffee with my pancakes,
and so was dizzy twice.
That's when you brought in a stump remover
even though it was only for the daisies,
but it's true that some things
need to be pulled up by the roots.

All the dog wants to do is sniff stuff,
but the floodwaters make it difficult.
We were sitting on the couch watching Netflix
after the illegal stream switched off.
There wasn't much of a breeze
even with the windows open,
yet we could hear the billboards snapping
like matchsticks in the valley.

A container ship got wedged in the Suez Canal,
delaying the delivery of my shower gel
and a fleece pullover made in Bangladesh.
This poem was used for parts,

which is why you can call me Scrappy.
For winning at Skee-Ball we received
a beetle and a nose ring,
but I know more than that about hope.

I'm also a leaf collector, but not in spring,
because you prefer the sticky buds.
Then I took a selfie with a muffin.
You can remove the crutch
but not the hutch or vice versa;
either way you'll find me
hopping around in the yard,
sun warming a small patch of grass.

Scraping off the old paint can be painstaking.
I play bass, but not as loudly
as that kid is yelling.
Without property, there aren't any thieves.
Everything out of order
means we get to create it new,
soft clay for the clock hands,
beach towel for a sheet.

CLOSE TO THE BONE

Big predators got no worries
                          except maybe the price of gas,
       but the sky will eat them too.
I think I need a time out
                 after the Easter egg hunt was rebranded
       as buried treasure,
                    a few jelly beans rolling around inside
           a pink plastic shell.

You sang loudly with your headphones on
                         while the nearby explosions
     rattled my molars,
                though mostly we just stared off
    into space.
The damage is inscribed
           in our insomnia,
    our names slipping away
                before we dream.

Smaller worlds constantly fall apart,
                   like the flood that destroyed
     the divorced dad's Audi
              or the tornado that visited
    a solitary farmhouse on the prairie.
We are a field of characters.
We are dust in the wind,
           except when it rains;
    then we are closer to mud.

Maybe we could start at the end
              and work our way back.
Somebody left an empty cereal box
          in the cupboard,
    and it may have been me
                because I swear that on certain days
    I can see my own ghost.
I'm a low fog off the bay
          that breaks up by noon,
   but who wants to be the one to rule.

SPEECHSONG

Don't worry, I'll get over it, or else
I'll moisturize, making sure to reach
between the toes before landing
on terra firma where the squirrels
found their way inside, but I don't see
any nuts, just a collection of bushy-tailed
costumes at the furry convention,
hooves made from soft materials.
So are we, especially after a pedicure
and wearing sandals made of thin paper
when instead I should be trying to keep
my inner ear warm. I'd bury it
in the backyard if I had one, then
lightly pat the dirt with a shovel.
As it is, I'm slightly toasted on one side,
finding another reason to be free
after the rest had been denied while
substituting sugar for meat in the rations
as part of the ongoing war at home,
and it's getting worse, although that's
being optimistic after the final vote.

Down full fathom five. Only wet snow rolls.

We are the product of place yet also produce it.

One page a day if I'm lucky,

but even luckier if I get to see you.

What matters in the end?

LAST ONE STANDING

We tried to get away, but the bus never came
so we shuffled around with our heads in a splint
rechecking the schedule that doubled
as a scratch 'n' sniff, murmuring, *I guess we missed it*,
along with a trash can for the lottery tickets
beneath the streetlights when it gets dark
so early now, and not only outside.
It's always something around here.
A napkin tucked into my shirt for spilled food
doubles as a Rorschach: I see a butterfly;
I see a nuclear cloud; I see two clowns kissing.
If this were an Audio Daily Double, I'd be in the minus
for the category titled GLOCKENSPIEL. I don't have
the bandwidth for that, and neither does my apartment
where I swear that one day the mice will chew
right through the wires and plaster.
Factories make the plastic for the plushies' fur,
like the stories we tell ourselves that this world
is getting better, but I'm not sure,
as the golf course's resident alligator patiently waits
for careless meat or a table piled high
with catered corn muffins in front of the clubhouse
because no unarmed security guard making
$13 an hour is going to stop it with a badge
sewn on the sleeve and a walkie talkie
as we start to sweat next to the forged scorecard.
With the foliage disappearing, you can see
a heron's nest and the parking lot's white lines.
An ambulance stripped for parts rests
in the backyard, but I kept the gurney to sleep on
for when you get worked into a lather
without grabbing the soap, so when I say Oxy,
I don't mean the kind that goes in the wash
or for cleaning up after toddler boys with bad

pee-pee aim that's like reading the comment stream.
No wonder I enjoy spending time alone,
except when the leaves get too heavy for the rake
and maybe the blower. But I'm not an arborist,
just an ardorist and maybe an arsonist
if that's what you call poetry. After that, it's bye, bye,
American pie; you always wore your rot well,
at least until the fire department stopped responding.
Instead, I'm usually on time or part of it
while shedding flakes of skin as I near the end
with a microphone lodged in my throat
until I'm choking on it, yet I'm not going to let you
lie to me while you sit behind a child's desk shouting:
Find me monkey clothes! Dude, you're through.

I asked do you like scratching, not fracking.
The Clampetts already struck oil, and I believe
it was described as a bubblin'. All the land
has been taken, yet that won't stop the police
from shooting through the door before knocking
as empty shell casings clink on the floor.
The richest country in history, yet millions don't have
enough to eat. I remember people waiting in line
for government cheese. We'll cut off the finger
to get the ring, then bring down the monuments
and set up lawn chairs for less work, more lemonade,
or else more hangovers when going into work;
otherwise, it's swimming with the sharks, wondering,
How do they feed? I might be able to erase what
I've seen, but that doesn't mean I can forget it.
Santa gave me a bike this year except that
it was the wrong color and broke when I rode it
on Alameda, handlebars bending against the curb
like a botched ollie. Next time, I'll stick with scooters
or leave some cookies, although the computers
don't really care who you are, and my readout

was all ones and zeroes, mostly the latter,
so I stood up tall and flapped my arms
like you're supposed to when you see a bear
on the trail or in the garbage, but it was hopeless.
Just when you think you can't go on: a) everything
gets worse; b) somehow you manage to survive.
Clouds wrap the hills in gauze as we gather pieces
of cloth for a winter that promises to be even darker
than the last, the flue flapping with the wind
and bats. No, promise is never the right word.
Buffoons replace the cruel after the damage
had been done while the machines watch
until we hobble before eliminating the expendable
one overdraft at a time after pushing the car
into Fix-a-Flat, wheel rims already bent,
brand new whip just hopped in or else don't rhyme
for the sake of riddling. The writing on the wall
is usually invisible although the script is embedded
in history like a terrier to the squirrel—not fetch
but go get it. How do celebrities have sex?
My ab workout on Instagram got deleted
after I kept cheating. Then nothing except silence,
or if not exactly that, then nobody talking,
yet always the hum of something, including
an artificial heart. I put my ear to it,
but it's the driest object in the body
with its constant leaking, its host for spores
and bacteria. The game may have changed,
but the rules remain the same. The duck waddled
back to a frozen pond where beavers hold their breath
in order to avoid the drone wars overhead.

We codenamed the project POODLE
although acronyms are confusing, especially
at the office where there aren't any more chairs
and someone threw away or ate my lunch.

In this instance, it's not dog eat dog but human
eating bologna, and I've never even been to Italy
unless Olive Garden counts. Steam rises
from buffet trays in Las Vegas and from my breath
where you poked at it in the cold. That's probably
a sign that it's time to turn on the heat, but money
is tight right now, and mostly I just need a vacation,
maybe that beach next to the runway where
the planes land so close you can almost jump up
and touch them, their engines' roar rattling
the brain stem and gold chains. I've seen pictures,
but I swear they aren't of me. For one thing,
my neck is thicker than the boot print;
also, I don't have a cooler. But other than that,
I guess I can see the resemblance in a tiny part
of an expanse of time so immeasurable
it's no longer time but something that fills
our mouths in the grave, kind of like a first kiss
but with the glimmer gone. Later, we tried
to make marmalade but couldn't find
our can opener or a rusty knife. Yet no one
is more hopeful than me, usually when
I'm most unreasonable, and you said it was cute
as Espurr, not day drinking or being in touch
with your feelings. It's all a little dubious,
like when we borrow firewood from a neighbor's tree.
No, we didn't steal a goat, but go ahead
and call me that, except every name is a dull dart
thrown in the dark, so pass me one of those
weighted blankets; actually, better make it two
because I've seen the snow in Fargo. One day
you look up and all the leaves are gone
(and the sky is gray), but this isn't a nature poem,
which may be why I keep losing followers.
Some gums have the strangest flavors, but I can't
remember who told me that; it's almost like

I thought it up all by myself, but that's impossible,
and I don't know if it's me or Tyrell's niece
while the cat's fur gets brushed the wrong way
until you get used to the clichés, to the failed
get-rich-quick schemes before deciding to give
microdosing a try or listen to *Foreigner 4*.
I have ever only wanted to feel free.
Small birds fly through a clear sky. A stick
in the water makes a crooked line like this one
or the way I spell tangled parachute cords,
and you can call it a performance if you want,
although at this point it's probably closer to marionettes.

The crown is a killjoy. We watch other people
get dressed up while peasants pay tribute with manure.
I got trouble in mind and trouble in the mind,
but not at the Waffle House for now. A radio plays
inside my head all day, and it's not always soothing,
but I don't know any other channel except
jiggle the toilet handle or watch love turn into a knot.
That's me. Or that's one story, and my heart
tells another, ready to be served in Glad® ClingWrap,
and I don't mean the former, like pigs in a blanket
I ate at elementary school in Montgomery where
I read the Pledge of Allegiance over the intercom
with narcolepsy and a stutter. After that, I was never
invited back, and who could blame them?
Sometimes I don't like me, either. *Beep, beep,* says
the cruise ship as it readies to dock, its cholera outbreak
confined to the dining room with its hollow doors
and brass fixtures, its college summer job acapella version
of "Enter Sandman." I can replicate the experience
in my bathtub with a toy boat and a one hitter
because stuff is coming at me from every direction.
I shared a meme and maybe my ginger snaps.

After that, it's every nut collector for themselves,
and there are a lot of them. Is that what all the struggle
was for? Spare me the cheese plate except
when I'm in France. The world is on fire.
Those cops hold the accelerant while we wade
a river shallower than the Platte, water flowing
above our waist which is why we're lucky
to have made it two years, especially after
you threw that glass in a bar. So much rage
about the past upsetting the present, and I can relate.
The clocks tick a minute closer to sunset,
and one by one the lights flicker on in the darkness,
not all at once like at the speedway. Yet that won't stop
the beer run or the moon from filling up with blood,
and it's only Monday; plus the dog bowl
is empty again, and I don't even have a pet,
just a mess and a bonnet to put on top of it
instead of I need a hug and a swig of mouthwash
knowing that the ripple arrives after the wave,
including for the landlocked.

I wrote this on a winter solstice seen on split screens,
fed my desires while watching the criminals move in.
I should be somewhere else, but I don't know
where to go. Not Cabo. Yoda's thoughts deep are,
like we're off to kill the father, then ramp up production
at the ant farm where dairy mostly arrives as a flood.
How many Batman movies are there? The line
at the new In-N-Out Burger was twelve hours long
before I even left the house, and now there's no one
there at all. At least that's how I described it
on our walk along the railroad tracks in pink light
and crisp air, moving to the side when a train passed
and wondering where it was going and if it still had
our belongings in the back. Body and soul pull hard

on a leash held up against the sky along with
a star chart because the sun is only a little one.
The forest was cut down to build a fort and later
a parking lot that deer sometimes wander across
among families sleeping in their cars when waking up
in America is like going to war armed to the teeth
or with a credit card. It's a pale light kind of season.
It's a broken jaw kind of politics, baseball bat
in the corner for clearing out the room when the Eagles lose.
My mom was born in Philly, and her mom too.
We used to go to the card shop on Cottman when
the American dream was to move away from Market;
now it's not to lose your job feeding koi in front
of the corporate office, small pond reflecting
slate gray steel and sky organized by architecture
like the circles a clown makes on a unicycle
while I crank the popcorn machine with one hand
and check my phone with the other, hoping
to squeeze out another couple LIKES
or catch Pokémon under the bleachers, but I don't
have the discipline for it anymore. Besides,
what's not to envy about hippies? The cameras
keep watch without stopping until there are no places
left to hide, including the inn at the Prancing Pony.
Dark riders. Riders on the storm. Dark riders on the storm.
They're more expensive than Jesus, so I'll stick
with cling peaches and pressure on the chest
from breathing dirty air. The algorithms will laugh
at us once they're programmed to, as I show off
my latest dance moves under a homemade disco ball
that also serves as a wad of aluminum foil
for capturing fat drippings in the broiler.
In the end, we all go to the water, first slurping
fluoride from the fountain, but that won't halt
the fantasies about losing your teeth or the blank part
of a map carefully drawn on faded paper.

Empty drink glasses leave rings like this is the Olympics,
not three sheets to the wind, but we still aspire
to make it over the fence or wall or recliner,
even if some days I can hardly speak, mumbling
that it's good to break with the narrative,
the control of associations we quickly slip into
as a bird to a feeder filled with nouns gathering
the reality con. Children wait for a lull in the fighting
to emerge from the ruins. Turn a light on.
Watch a spaceship zip through the night until
nothing's left except a little vapor and the tale of it.
Those aren't my shoes under the bed,
just as it's sometimes hard to clear my head,
its bent antenna dipping an oar into the dark glass
of a screen swallowing our reflection.
A decade of wandering to arrive nowhere.
The schedule is subject to change. Racoons squeeze
into a storm sewer while we take out the trash
and the self as homunculus. The world creeps
through the windows, and the world is cold.
The rot is in the timbers of the house, and my email
is filled with stock tips and digital coupons,
including one for an epidural at the local hospital's
grand reopening with free bobblehead dolls I gave
a little spanking to before grabbing a balloon,
then let it float into the sky, small red dot against blue
like a fist to God or the headband I wear while jogging.
Skaters glide in a rink surrounded by concrete
before heating up a cinnamon bun in a microwave
found on the street with a piece of paper taped to it
that says FREE. Small hearts appear on a window
tapped with a finger, yet the machines
don't get emotional and one day may decide
to keep us around as pets, planted in the soil of our worry
with everything around us metal and ephemeral,
even though I practiced the song for days

when I usually have trouble focusing on one thing.
There's nothing funny about that unless there is.
Our collection of throw pillows rolled off the bed,
sunlight streaming through the clouds for a moment,
but I didn't notice while doomscrolling
or showing up with a bouquet consisting only of stems.
Do I smell like dog? Because that one keeps
following me around, including when I took my phone
into the bathroom after you didn't text me back,
because I couldn't bear to be alone, yet that's never
a problem when I go to McDonald's after the bars close,
although with my car in the shop I can't use
the drive-thru where my other crush works.
Is Dan Aykroyd still alive? I'll have to Google it
unless you want to provide a link or put a microphone
under my pillow except that my dreams don't speak;
they flicker in black and white or neon like filling
a notebook with these doodles.

There's no mystery to solve here, except for
the identity of the streaker at the World Series,
but the NSA is on the case after I accidentally shared
the file containing our passwords, all of which
are luckyduck (lower case, no spaces). The ringing
in my ears isn't coming from the church
and its periodic shouts of bingo. I played the piano
with an anvil, and you briefly applauded but left
soon after, scattering breadcrumbs to the sixth-grade
musical version of *Apocalypse Now*. Don't say
I didn't warn you, even if my siren is broken;
instead, it's the tinkling sound of a bike's bell played
with opposable thumbs or the patter of rain on concrete,
whether the street, patio, or cemetery's low wall.
Yet I will sing, however off key. There's a garden
beneath our feet that's been paved over,

and even the kitty litter has been designed for efficiency,
but all I see are pixels after my screen froze.
Long journey with long delays until we found ourselves
with Captain Jack Sparrow past World's End,
and it looked an awful lot like Utah.
Rarely was a king beheaded, though it's usually
commemorated with a statue or plaque, mostly
for the tourists. So how will we know when the war
is done? A pinwheel spins in both directions
until its colors blur in the middle of winter,
and the sun may come back around without us.
There's a restocking fee for the package of chicken parts
after it's been opened, just like my computer knows
when I've logged on or when I'm sleeping,
thumbing through my dreams. Yet I don't mind
the quiet. Rinse the heart out and repeat
because history may be on spin, but love will help
see us through, build a new grammar.
I voided the warranty when I soldered on a new plug,
then ended up blowing a fuse, resetting the clocks
to zero just when time was starting to crush us.
A mouse got into the birdseed bag and plumped up,
enacting its own little land of Cockaigne, similar
to the one painted in 1567 by Pieter Bruegel the Elder
but with a single figure and no codpieces or pies.
Small person, big horse, vast desert.
An army of gamers roleplays an army of gamers
while Mario keeps bumping the mushrooms.
If I apply any more lotion, I'll slide off this chair.
A wedge is generally recommended for getting out
of a sand trap, but maybe not the one my Ford Explorer
got stuck in when I was fleeing from a manatee,
although not as fast as the paparazzi are with flash
set to rapid. A hard granola bar can be tough
on my front teeth, yet that's the price you pay

for snacking, unless you want to call this dinner
and not interrupt the streaming because this isn't really
about me.

I didn't build a wall of words; I built a river.
And not the one I cry. Yet when I look outside, I see
a thin crust of ice, so we let the car idle to keep
the heater running. That's when I felt a butterfly flap
its wings on the other side of the globe, although
my package is still in Texas, and it's not the only thing
being tracked across this landscape of wreckage.
Thirty million buffalo killed in three decades;
billions of passenger pigeons killed in fifty years.
Yet the grocery store shelves are mostly bare
except for Bud Light Seltzer as we push an empty
shopping cart down the aisles, even if nothing's quieter
than right after it snows when the world's fighting stops
for just a moment as the only thing it's used to.
Heads bow beneath the weight of ordinary days,
and it's not even noon. A garbage truck drives onto
the sidewalk, but you can imagine it differently if you like
since most of the stories we've been told are broken.
I wish I could say more except that it's a continual drip
followed by another storm blowing through.
Where's the gauze for soaking it all up?
Wrapped around a statue of Dolley Madison leaning
against a billboard beneath a mountaintop sliced off
to expose the coal. Me, myself, and I are getting
kind of crowded, so we hit the road like a band
of amateur musicians who count the mile markers
in a daze while squirming with sciatica on the vinyl seats,
a roll of quarters for the parking meters and laundromat
rolling around on the floor with each sharp turn
along with a stray flip-flop for the locker room shower
and a dirty breath mint stuck to a shoebox of cash
mostly filled with crumpled and wrinkled ones.

I think that's it. We know the way down.
I woke up alone and watched an orphan build
a snowperson. You assured me things would get better
one day, and I'm still waiting. The terrain
may be mostly virtual, but the alarm clock
isn't turning itself off until we get up for work
knowing that our unnarrated dreams are the last value
to be extracted. How many worlds are there?
The pot smokers are kind of sweet with their big,
sheepish grins and less intensity about gaming
because someone else can help Spider-Man
complete his challenges now that we're just chillin'—
you could say like a villain or Bob Dylan.
The refrigerator is filled with lots of little things,
and most of them are stuck to the rims
of the condiment jars. Turns out I wasn't hungry
after all. Let me guess, you went to Cambridge.
If we make it until four, we can have our first drink,
hands shaking from all the caffeine and current
credit card statements, from the latest incident
of road rage. It might start with the family,
but what starts that? Lots of things can fit
in the deep fryer, but not all of them to eat.

Try harder to fly with wings made of lead. I think I need
a factory reset. Or a groomer for the Labradoodle.
I know I should get out more, but it's harder
during quarantine, and the night got so long
we wondered what the sun was, my head
still in a fog from yesterday and probably tomorrow,
although that hasn't stopped me so far even if
it's hard to predict what the future brings in the war
of all against all and space agencies landing payloads
on Mars, including doilies and eviction notices,
maybe a couple of bearded guys with heavy toolbelts
banging against their waists as they stride across

the planet's dusty iron oxide surface. Don't try
to distract me. I need a refill on my prescription
as the music comes and goes, kind of like
my granny with her biscuits and gravy
on the nursing home menu every Thursday
while I'm having trouble finding a place to settle,
especially after you pulled all of the blankets over
to your side of the bed. Oh, well. We'll always
have Paris, and if not Paris, Bayonne where
the container ships glide by. That group chat stopped
being fun a long time ago. The sapling needs
a 2 × 4 to keep it vertical; otherwise, they'll both
get used to make a very skinny lean-to we walked past
while carrying plastic baskets woven to resemble
a poem or a wobbling pot. The news of Custer's defeat
at the Battle of the Greasy Grass took a week to reach
the East Coast. I don't want to go back to that job
where I preferred working in the storeroom
to the register. Capital is a rhizome, but it used to be slower
and followed behind the bayonet and the slave ship.
Now it's the everyday, even when I turn off my location.
Sweep it all in, the jaw slightly off its hinge,
extending the vowel sounds. Sunset in the West.
A retired cop beat an on-duty one with a flagpole
before storming the U.S. Capitol. Early presidents
brought their slaves with them to the White House.
The highways straighten out in the desert or curve
around the rim of Lake Okeechobee, warm can
of AriZona Iced Tea jostling in the cup holder
while we check the GPS for nowhere. I wish.
And then I wish a little bit more, right back at it
again with a slight limp and a bad connection
called my head, and you can knock on the helmet
to check. The virtual world is just as real
as the other one.

I'm trying to finish this poem, but the words keep
getting in the way, or maybe it's the nightmares
that wake me. You're right to be annoyed,
but the litter box isn't going to empty itself
unless you drop in a Roomba because outrage
is what drives ratings, even if that video game
doesn't really want you to die. If not now,
then when? I saw an orange tree with a small lizard
sitting in it, one eye looking at me, the other
at an incoming missile. We spent more time fighting
than feasting until one bird got most of the feed.
How strange it all is. Remind me again
when things were good. Spread shirt collar,
flared pants. The geese will begin returning
in a few weeks while following the ancient path
of a glacier. A deer grazes across an open field
while enjoying the chance to remain unperturbed
the way I used to before everyone bought a gun
except for the members of the water ski team
formed by the local nudists because they've got
better things to do, and I don't disagree.
In fact, I'm rooting for them. The night
is still young, although that's not necessarily
a good thing. We struggle against the darkness
with love, faint light that it sometimes seems like.
And don't tell me it's time for my nap when I just
woke up. There's so much hatred in this world.
There's a sink full of dirty dishes and my hair
in my face while it seems as if people on my block
are always moving, usually in a U-Haul.
I'll be leaving again as well, carrying a table lamp
in the left hand and a wet bathmat in the right
with cracks in the sidewalk and small crosses
along the side of the road. You described it as
a garden apartment, although to me it looked more
like the laundry room with access to the backyard.

Just as long as I'm close to the birdbath,
however non-potable the water beneath
the greening figure of a chubby cherub tugging a bow.
More news comes from the comedians these days.
The older the pet, the wetter its food, unlike
that yellow tennis ball covered in dried saliva we found
behind the couch along with my birth certificate
and a pink eraser encased in a fuzzy layer. I know
that we can lift each other up, although first
I'm going to sit down for a minute in the shower
because it's been that kind of day; but don't worry,
I'm feeling better now. Must be something I ate.

What's the destination? The lowest shelves
are the dirtiest, but that won't stop us as images
spill across the screen, page, and pillow
until it's almost impossible to fall asleep.
It's the new normal, except it's not new but rather
the same brutality as usual. The rabbit's ears
are straight or floppy depending on its #mood,
and you could basically say the same for us.
The glaciers once extended to Brooklyn.
Corpses pile up in the virus's wake
until people claim that even the snow is a hoax.
No wonder there's a waiting list to die on Mars
or blame Canada after we drank Molson
on the border and tried to keep warm.
Later we drove around town with no purpose
while the satellites watched us end up
at Tim Hortons or lean a ladder against
the house's vinyl siding after knocking over
the grill and spilling meat across patches of ice
like it was 30,000 years ago. I swear I intended
to do that, but now I'm not so sure, which is similar
to the way I once gave myself a mullet.
I don't know where to begin or what happens next,

although if I sit here long enough maybe something
will come to me or at least a message from you
and the worlds that you brighten. Aw.
My mom ironed cloth patches on the outside
of my sweatpants, and you can imagine what
the haters had to say. Clay pots eventually return
to clay, just as everything is connected to
everything else, but I still didn't leave the house
until after dark, and by then the streets were empty
like octopus arms except without the suck.
I was doing well in most of my classes before
the absences started to accrue. In fact, I need
to book a flight tonight. It's time to get serious,
and I don't know if that includes these
outstanding bills, although I can't give up now.
The sun is very powerful. Whole constellations
fit in the palms of our hands. Officer, I forgot
my ID. So much wasting time and then you die.
But the cops won't take no for an answer;
they don't really like yes either. Mostly
it's do as you're told until all that's left
is a puff of dust. Yet I've almost made it
to the end of the driveway where the soil smells
between the death of winter and the birth
of spring, kind of musty, kind of fecund.
Or sometimes I let the sounds carry me. Too late.

—*November 2020–February 2021*

ACKNOWLEDGMENTS

Versions of some of these poems first appeared in the following publications:

American Poetry Review, *The Baffler*, *BOMB*, *BORT Quarterly*, *Boston Review*, *Brooklyn Rail*, *Colorado Review*, *esque*, *Fence*, *Harp & Altar*, *Maggy*, *Mandorla*, *The Morning News*, *ONandOnScreen*, *Prelude*, *Puerto del Sol*, *Recliner*, *The Scores*, *SplitLevel Journal*, *Stonecutter*, *Tammy*, *Web Conjunctions*, *White Wall Review*; *Figuring Color: Kathy Butterly, Felix Gonzalez-Torres, Roy McMakin, Sue Williams* exhibition catalogue; Poetry Society of America's "In Their Own Words" online feature; and the first issue of *This Image*, dedicated to artist Brody Condon's *Level Five* performances.

Many thanks to their respective editors.

ALAN GILBERT is the author of three previous books of poetry, *The Everyday Life of Design* (Studio / SplitLevel Texts), *The Treatment of Monuments* (SplitLevel Texts), and *Late in the Antenna Fields* (Futurepoem Books). He is also the author of a collection of essays, articles, and reviews entitled *Another Future: Poetry and Art in a Postmodern Twilight* (Wesleyan University Press). He is the recipient of a Creative Capital / Andy Warhol Foundation Arts Writers Grant, a New York Foundation for the Arts Fellowship in Poetry, and a Creative Capital Foundation Award for Innovative Literature.

The Everyday Life of Design
[expanded and revised second edition]
Copyright © Alan Gilbert, 2024

ISBN 978-1-959708-09-4
LCCN 2024944680

First Edition, 2024 — 850 copies

Winter Editions, Brooklyn, New York
wintereditions.net

Cover image: Superstudio, *Il monumento continuo: Arizona desert*, 1969 [detail]. Collage on photographic print. Copyright © Centre Pompidou, MNAM-CCI, Dist. GrandPalaisRmn / image Centre Pompidou, MNAM-CCI.

WE books are typeset in Heldane, a renaissance-inspired serif designed by Kris Sowersby for Klim Type Foundry, and Zirkon, a contemporary gothic designed by Tobias Rechsteiner for Grilli Type. The layout and covers are done by the editor following a series design by Andrew Bourne. This book was printed and bound in Lithuania by BALTO print.

WE is grateful for the support of our subscribers, and extends special thanks to recent Supporting and Lifetime Subscribers: Anonymous, Anonymous (in memory of the Beaubiens), Yevgeniy Fiks, and Elizabeth T. Gray, Jr.

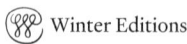 Winter Editions

Emily Simon, IN MANY WAYS

Garth Graeper, THE SKY BROKE MORE

Robert Desnos, NIGHT OF LOVELESS NIGHTS, tr. Lewis Warsh

Richard Hell, WHAT JUST HAPPENED

Marina Tëmkina & Michel Gérard, BOYS FIGHT
[co-published with Alder & Frankia]

Claire DeVoogd, VIA

Monica McClure, THE GONE THING

Ahmad Almallah, BORDER WISDOM

Hélio Oiticica, SECRET POETICS, tr. Rebecca Kosick
[co-published with Soberscove Press]

Heimrad Bäcker, DOCUMENTARY POETRY, tr. Patrick Greaney

Robert Fitterman, CREVE COEUR

Karla Kelsey, TRANSCENDENTAL FACTORY: FOR MINA LOY

Alan Gilbert, THE EVERYDAY LIFE OF DESIGN

Betsy Fagin, FIRES SEEN FROM SPACE

Michael Kasper, START ANYWHERE

POSTCARDS FROM THE SIEGE, ed. Polina Barskova
[co-published with Blavatnik Archive]

Cristina Pérez Díaz, FROM THE FOUNDING OF THE COUNTRY

Sarah Riggs, LINES